THIS OLD CHURCH

This Old Church

THE INDISPENSABLE GUIDE FOR
RESTORING CHURCH BUILDINGS

I O N   G R U M E Z A

RESOURCE *Publications* · Eugene, Oregon

In memory of my father,

LEON GRUMEZA,

who spent countless days

repairing his church

in a Romanian village

Resource Publications
A division of Wipf and Stock Publishers
199 W 8th Ave, Suite 3
Eugene, OR 97401

This Old Church
The Indispensable Guide for Restoring Church Buildings
By Grumeza, Ion
Copyright©2005 Pilgrim Press
ISBN 13: 978-1-60899-180-8
Publication date 11/10/2009
Previously published by Pilgrim Press, 2005

CONTENTS

P r e f a c e

❀

This book is the product of more than fifteen years of my helping restore some twenty-five churches. The process included working with church committees and their members, as well with people outside the church, such as architects, building engineers, building inspectors, town officials, independent contractors, interior decorators, and many others.

How did I come to this line of work and what exactly do I do?

My introduction to this business was accidental. In the 1980s, I was a real estate agent. As is often the case, I was asked by clients if I knew repairmen or contractors who could work on their houses before the owners listed them, or who could repair, restore, or remodel houses that had just been purchased. As it happened, I had worked in construction as a young man growing up in Romania. I had even helped my parents construct their house. So I had a sound, basic knowledge of many labor skills to which I added the understanding of what works and what doesn't work that comes with experience in the real estate business.

I began small, by recommending handymen, small crews of workers, and various contractors I knew who did good work. Before long, my priest learned about my new line of work and asked me to refinish the entrance doors of our 150-year-old church. This $3,000 job led to additional work, and nine months later I found myself involved with $200,000 worth of major restorations in the church. A small article in the local newspaper described my work, and I subsequently found myself a "church restoration expert," the person to call for any church job.

From the beginning, my role was to locate workers who were reliable and proficient, and then to find contractors who would bid for major jobs. I often chose people who had come to America from eastern Europe; they worked in the old-fashioned ways, relying more on their skills than on modern tools. For instance, they had far more expertise in plaster and stucco work than locally trained workers. Since churches built a century or more ago were predominantly built of plaster and stucco, this gave me an advantage when it came to job proposals, and eventually won us many bids.

So my job was and still is to match the best working crew to the particular job—and to interface with church committees and everyone involved in the restoration from the earliest planning phase through the completion of the work. My first duty as a church restoration agent is to find a church that needs repairs. I am happy to say that in many cases, it is the church that finds me. Having credentials is important; I have a track record and many churches that can be checked for references. As with any construction project, it is important to find someone who has proven expertise and reliability.

Part of my job is to do the necessary investigations to identify problems and then write a "scope of work" proposal outlining what is needed to correct those problems. This document becomes the basis for a contract that additionally contains recommendations from architects, engineers, and other experts in diverse fields.

So far I have acted as a planner and an estimator for the church. Unless I am awarded the contract, my "scope of work" proposal and the estimates are used for the bidding process. Because my numbers are known, it puts me at a relative disadvantage since the other bidding contractors can find out the work and costs that I have proposed. Still, church committees often do not take the lowest bid—rather, they go with the bid that they feel ensures the best work for the money. Because of that important consideration, I have won many bids for my contractors, whose good reputations help me get the job for both of us.

Once we have a signed contract, my dual role begins: keeping both the contractor and the church people happy during the entire restoration work. My being the "go-between" eliminates any direct confrontations between the workers and the church supervisors. Because I have no personal ego involved in this dialogue, I can be impartial and convey the exact message from one end of the chain of command to the other. I also understand the concerns of each, and I do my best to address the problems, not the individuals. This allows me to build credibility and trust and to keep the job running on a time- and cost-efficient course.

RESTORATION STEP BY STEP

A glimpse at the table of contents will show you what this book is about: it provides a step-by-step outline for restoration, with time-proven working "recipes."

To guarantee a happy ending for any restoration project, it is important to understand how contractors and the people who hire them perceive their duties and ways of conducting themselves. Often the person who is hands-on is liable to lose sight of the big picture and can even focus so much on minute details that he or she loses control of the overall working picture.

On the other hand, the one overseeing that person may see *only* the big picture, missing crucial details that can lead to unanticipated and unavoidable problems.

It is crucial that Restoration Committee members step in to coordinate the numerous steps of restoration projects. All the practical issues described in this book come from verifiable experiences, backed by the comments and advice I learned in real situations. The steps and examples can serve as your guide to anticipating and preventing unpleasant and costly occurrences and, equally important, to ensuring a safe working environment.

This book describes the logical procedures to be followed before, during, and after restoration, with easy-to-comprehend tips for the various phases of a complicated and costly project. Because it is the first book on this subject, I have included many of my personal experiences as illustrations, so the reader can use them to anticipate and recognize the issues. I hope it will be of some comfort to know that most of what goes wrong is not because someone is at fault, but more likely because it happens often and to so many in similar circumstances. In other words, expect the unexpected, no matter how prepared you think you are. When a restoration project involves tens of people, hundreds of thousands of dollars, and the interests of local officials and the entire community, it is helpful to have a guide on how to go about the work and what may happen along the way.

HOW RESTORATION COMMITTEES CAN BEST USE THIS BOOK

From the squeaky floors to the crumbling towers and from peeling paint to the falling ceiling, parishioners love to talk about any restoration work, as many have already had similar experiences with their own homes. But to move from talking to action is a long and costly road. Proper planning of any restoration work is a must to ensure good results. Such planning requires many groups of competent people.

There is no doubt that all committees want to do the right thing for their church. The members are all well-intentioned, and some bring helpful skills and experiences to the table. Yet each individual needs to work as part of a coordinated team, and that is sometimes easier said than done. This book is designed to help bring all parties together by clarifying issues and providing guidelines for how best to accomplish what needs to be done.

Ideally, the first thing each committee member should do is read this book almost like a homework assignment before going to the first meeting of the Restoration Committee. If all have read the book, they already have something in common: they have a better understanding of the process, no matter what the specifics of the job may be. Moreover, each chapter addresses a specific restoration topic and serves as a guide when the committee is facing a dilemma or a problem. Committee members may open the book to a particular page and read exactly what they need to know. Most important, with this common knowledge the rest of the committee members can do the same, and an agreement is much more likely to be in the making.

This book can serve as a learning tool or as validation of what it is already known. However, just like any dictionary, where each word has more than one meaning, parts of this book also can be the subject of interpretation. Dealing with people involves dealing with their emotions. Dealing with money involves dealing with strict responsibilities. Dealing with a job that needs to be done properly requires working skills, careful planning, and deadlines.

This book covers important issues in a logical and practical manner. It is a primer for anyone involved in church restoration. It describes traditional ways of solving many common problems. Your contractor may have other suggestions that are equally viable and take advantage of the latest material and procedures. Many of the steps can also be easily applied to antique or vintage houses or other old buildings.

The reader should go through each chapter to identify the problem his or her church has, and then spend more time with the needed chapter. Match the chapter with the problem. If the church needs a new roof, pay special attention to the roof section. If the roof leaks have already affected other parts of the church, then go back and read more about those problems and how to solve them. Regardless of the specific chapter you need, read the one dealing with "politics," for it will teach you how to judge things you do not see but are there and make a strong impact on the job.

It is my wish to satisfy the needs and expectations of a Restoration Committee, which was the motivation to write this book in the first place.

ACKNOWLEDGMENTS

I offer thanks and appreciation to Brothers Antique & Vintage Restorations and the other antique and vintage restoration craftspeople with whom I have worked and who did the enduring, quality work reflected in the text and photographs of this book.

Introduction

THE CHURCH BUILDING IN AMERICA

The history of churches in America is relatively new compared to the history of churches in Europe and temples in Asia, but American church builders retained the designs of the western world influenced by Emperor Hadrian's basilica of the second century c.e.

As Christian leaders gained power, their churches increased accordingly in size and architectural luxury. During the Middle Ages, the architectural design of the church influenced that of the castle and vice versa. Imposing buildings of military architecture were surrounded by walls and moats, as well as by the dwellings of common people seeking their protection. There was one major difference between castles and churches: castles were inaccessible to the commoners, while churches invited all inside.

The decline of the castle made room for palaces that greatly influenced the elegant architecture of the church. Yet the church remained basically one huge, open room. To ensure the safety of that sizeable room, a special construction technique was developed to hold the immense roof and high walls in place. In addition to the buttresses and supporting columns, elaborate arches and arcades were built to imply the imagined magnitude of heaven, while also holding the entire building together.

With thousands of workers available to build castles, castles were built quickly. But with just a handful of people, often mainly monks, it took many years to build a church, an abbey, or a cathedral, making each structure a great labor of love. The proud and monumental churches have lasted, however, while many castles are today mere ghostly ruins.

The best minds and the best craftsmen of the time created an ecclesiastical architecture, equally beautiful outside and inside, commanding instant respect and encouraging pious feelings. The ever-growing towers continually amazed the dwarfed people who saw the church as God's dwelling. The towers served as observation posts for townspeople to look out for enemies and fires; the bells announced the times for religious services or curfews. Later, clocks were installed to mark the passing of time.

While castles crumbled into ruins and palaces moved to secluded places, churches were conveniently erected in the middle of communities. The church, easily accessible, was the anchor of daily life. The minister was perceived as God's servant, and so were the priest and the reverend, all called "father" to show respect for their wisdom and spiritual role.

Because churches were unlikely to be attacked, their doors and windows reached heavenly proportions, decorated to create a religious mood. Churches always inspired the arts, and artists never stopped beautifying them. Sculptures, paintings on the walls, and stained glass were indeed the closest vision of divinity, the only one a mortal could come close to.

With no trained architects, and workers who did not know how to read or write, the magnificent churches were built by trial and error. No one knows how many of them collapsed before being completed. But the ones that lasted are marvels of engineering skills—modern architects cannot fully explain their complicated structures. For over one thousand years, Europeans constantly built miracles of glorious constructions filled with artistic masterpieces to enhance the noble mission of these edifices.

❁

The history of church architecture in America is less glamorous but equally rich in tradition and style. Considering that the first churches were built after 1600, mostly in the cradle of Massachusetts, amazing progress was made in just four hundred years.

Within the first settlements, a "meeting house" was vital and the same space was used for religious purposes as well. The term "meeting house" persists to our day because, indeed, people must meet to worship God in one voice.

The first churches were built by sailors with the same methods they used to build their boats. A similar architectural design to that of boats was applied, especially for the roof configuration. It is not unusual to find an "ark" or a "ship church" along the ocean shores where the colonizers landed. The mast, built to collect wind power into the sails, was replaced with the spire intended to reach out to the mysteries of the sky.

A sizeable church could be built in just one to three years and cost less than $5,000, bell included. The earliest churches were built from wood, abundantly found yards away from the construction sites. Wood was a less expensive material than stone and brick, faster to use in building, and it held up better in the damp oceanic environment.

For unknown reasons, entire forests of chestnut trees began to die some two hundred years ago, and churches of that period, especially in the New England area, were built entirely with wood from those trees. This wood was not only a most enduring construction material, but it was also beautiful and easy to work with. The happy coincidence produced countless churches that lasted in pristine condition to the present.

By the end of the eighteenth century, stone and brick were used, primarily in the cities where these materials were easier to procure. The nature of these materials allowed the churches to achieve impressive sizes and heights.

Some of the churches were built by unskilled volunteers with little help from architects or master-builders. Yet these structures remain colonial masterpieces to this day. Designed through necessity and built with practicality, they are not showpieces, but they shaped the American church style.

The British, French, Germans, Russians, and Scandinavians created their own distinctive church style, and so did the Americans. The American church style is open and simple, mostly without luxurious oil paintings and complicated woodwork. Even so, it carries a powerful iconographic theme.

The new architecture found a harmony of lines between human-built structure and people's understanding of God's nature. It provided a simple but comfortable place for contemplation about humanity's short-lived role on earth and passing deeds. It radiated purity, warmth, peace, confidence, and spiritual meditation about the mystery never solved: the creation of humankind in the universe.

Unlike in Europe, where famous crusaders, royalty, or bishops are buried in the heavily ornate tombs outside the church, American sanctuaries carry no such historical testimonies. They do, however, shelter spiritual shrines for the common people.

Like veritable national monuments, the early American churches were placed on high elevations or hilltops. They faced the sea or large plazas left open in front of them. Nearly every community in America has a Church Street, even if the church itself is no longer present.

Soon parish houses and rectories were built to accommodate the clergy and their families. These structures were built with the same sturdiness and elegant craftsmanship that defined the colonial style. The Catholic Church, on the other hand, followed the traditional Romanesque style found in churches in large European cities. Gothic and Greek Revival treatments found their way into the lavish designs of the new churches.

By the beginning of the twentieth century, the ethnic style of the Russian or Greek Orthodox churches, as well as that of the synagogues and mosques, provided architectural diversity. But the Puritan-colonial style continued to dominate the church landscape of America with plenty of room for the varying styles of other religions and denominations.

I

B U I L D I N G   R E S T O R A T I O N :
W H A T   I S   I T
A N D   W H Y   D O   I T ?

LOVE THY CHURCH

Any church has a long history of use, spanning many years, many generations, and many changes over time. In spite of what happens in the world, the church seems to outlast humans and events—evidence of its eternal role. But its structure is not eternal, and it needs periodic reinforcement—or at least a close preventive inspection, especially if the building is older than one hundred years.

Church structures last longer than houses because they are used only a few times a week and only a few hours each time. Also, compared to houses, churches are built by the best craftsmen with the best of materials and with a generous budget to take care of each de-

5

tail. The prime location of churches further ensures optimum building grounds and solid foundations.

Unlike homes, inside the church there are rituals and disciplines that reduce abuse of the building and prolong its life. But what is a plus in terms of the building not being abused is also a negative: the lack of permanent occupancy means there is no one to watch the building all the time, and minor problems are likely to go undetected for years. Eventually they become major problems and, when finally detected, they can be a serious threat to the building and even to the parishioners.

When do you know it's time for restoration? Usually it is when everyone notices the leak marks on the ceiling and along the walls, loose plaster hanging from the ceiling or walls, or water pooling inside the building. Certainly these are red flags and indicate that it's time to start talking about repair.

Like everything made by humans, the church has its limits of endurance when facing the passing time. The reasons are many, and some important ones are listed below:

- The large size of the church structure allows settling that affects the original angles of the roof line, supporting walls, door and window frames, etc.
- Large, tall, and heavy towers lean against the church, pushing its structure away from its original lines.
- Numerous roof layers make the structure crumble under their weight.
- Materials used in construction, usually the mortar, which was made of what we would now consider inferior quality components, undergo a natural decay.
- The old wood was never treated with preservatives, allowing for insects and humidity that cause decay.
- Natural elements took their toll over the years, especially on the north side of the church.
- Earthquakes and other natural disasters may have caused serious hidden safety problems in addition to the obvious damage.

- A long history of water damages never fully repaired may make the plaster and stucco separate from ceiling and walls.
- Portions of the foundation shift out of alignment, sinking corners or tilting the building.
- Floors and stairs move under the weight of parishioners, noisily signaling an inevitable collapse.

Typically at this point no one is aware that in all likelihood there is much more happening. What is seen is only a small piece of the total problem, for, in fact, the building may be falling apart!

Detecting problems is therefore the first reason people begin a restoration project. But restoration is also for preventing problems before they start and for further beautifying the church. Prevention is the key word when fixing or redoing something before is too late, when the building crumbles. Simply put, it saves the church from further deterioration.

WHEN SHOULD REPAIRS BEGIN?

There is no better time than *now* to do something about those obvious signs of deterioration, before they become bigger, harder to fix, and more costly.

There are many levels of improvement, and it is important to identify which is right for your church:

- **Repairs** are the most common measures, so as to immediately fix what may harm the building and prevent further damages. Any work in this category is considered an emergency.
- **Preservation,** as the dictionary indicates, is work performed to keep something from decaying. In our case, it refers to maintaining the building in its original state by proper maintenance.
- **Rehabilitation,** or reconditioning, is aimed at reinforcing the building structure and upgrading the use of it without changing the original architectural style.
- **Remodeling** is to modernize the building and may affect the look of the church, inside and outside.

- ☙ **Restoration** is the re-creation of the building by making it stronger while replacing missing parts so as to retain the original style. It is a major work that reclaims at least the outer original appearance of the church.

- ☙ **Historical restoration** involves the scholarly duplication of the character of the original building, including interior decorations and furniture appropriate to the era in which the church was first constructed. This is likely to involve removing later additions to the main building.

To the preceding dry definition of restoration, many other subjective meanings can be attached.

The emotional factor is always on the top of the list. Regardless of how palatial or humble our church is, to us it is the most beautiful because of the vivid memories and emotions that are attached to it. In many cases, it is the place where images of our grandparents and many other relatives or friends come to mind during our meditation. Things are as they always have been there, so our feelings about our loved ones flow readily. To restore the church is to preserve those memories.

The church reflects our way of life. It is where we celebrate birth, marriage, and death, where our children learn faith and values. To restore the building is in fact to restore the connection with God and heavenly expectations and pass them along to other generations.

2

FORMING THE CHURCH RESTORATION COMMITTEE

The first step in church restoration is assembling a Restoration Committee. The committee is important for several reasons. First, it is too big a job to ask just one person to deal with all the issues and details. Furthermore, leaving all the decisions to one person is akin to allowing him or her to become a "restoration dictator." It is a common joke that if you want to delay action, you should form a committee. But in the case of a Restoration Committee, the concept is a blessing: it usually brings together people who are willing to work hard, are experienced at getting things done, and want things done in an efficient and effective manner.

A Restoration Committee ideally has at least five members. Typically it includes a treasurer, vestry members, and property trustees, as well as active or retired architects, building engineers, contractors, financial advisors, and decorating professionals, among others. One should be designated the chairperson, coordinating all activities. I recommend the chair *not* be the church pastor, so as to be spared having to choose sides during the inevitable quarrels that arise during restoration planning and the actual work. It is, however, extremely helpful to have the pastor present during important restoration meetings. After all, he or she is the one who will live with the restoration decisions and their results. The pastor's opinions must be carefully considered, for they may be well-substantiated with vital facts for church activity.

Once the committee is formed, it must check with the National Register of Historic Places about the status of the building. All restoration work will be determined by the church's standing, and any planning must be in compliance with state guidelines.

The best ideas come from those who search for old pictures or sketches and historical references, who study the era during which the church was originally constructed, and who try to protect its authenticity. This is an ideal job for members of the Restoration Committee. Please note: I recommend not relying on architects for these ideas: they tend to have limited time for each project and are likely to have no previous church restoration experience. I am not suggesting ignoring their help, however. To the contrary, architects' input is crucial to designing building enforcements and finding ways to avoid damaging the existing vintage elements. Architects also know how to camouflage modern equipment: ducts for heating, ventilation, and air conditioning (HVAC), pipes, radiators, and other visually offensive fixtures. In addition, many town halls require detailed architectural blueprints before granting building permits for restoration.

No two churches are alike and no standardized building rules can be applied to all old churches. Unlike most houses, there are no predictable or usual measurements to deal with. From the size of the studs and their spacing, to the shape of the windows or the roof, everything is unique. Therefore each restoration job is a new challenge for committee members and ultimately for the contractor.

3

IDENTIFYING YOUR BUILDING'S PROBLEMS

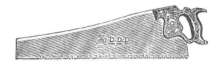

The Restoration Committee is charged with realistically assessing the extent of restoration needed, weighing the expense, and prioritizing the tasks. Its members should keep in mind that the major restoration of a church occurs once in a hundred years. Their mission is to ensure the historical and religious value of the church.

Just like an old person who experiences various health problems, the vintage church shows signs of deterioration. The Restoration Committee, not to mention other parishioners and townspeople, have noted the shabby appearance and very likely have already itemized many of the visible flaws: an over-patched roof, flashings that are out of line, peeling paint, crooked walls, rotten wood, a crumbling foundation, and so on. But to detect the root of any problem requires going beyond the visual impression, and here the Restoration Committee steps up to the plate.

Having already checked with the National Register of Historic Places, and while committee members are researching historical documents on the church, the Restoration Committee prepares an Inspection Checklist. Please note that it is crucial to take extensive and accurate notes and photographs throughout the inspection process. The checklist should include:

- The building's walls: Identify why they are out of plumb line or why they undulate. Horizontal cracks in the outside or inside walls are reliable red flags signaling walls that are on the verge of collapsing.

- The windows: Check on whether the windows and doors still have right angles and whether they still close and open with ease. If there are problems with the windows and doors, it is likely that the building structure itself is weak.

- Wood siding and trim: These can bulge or be loosely attached, covered by rot, mold, or mildew; trim may be out of line, while caulking and painting may be cracked and falling off.

- The sides of the building: If the structure has been slightly tilted for the past fifty or more years, there is weight settlement.

- The roof: Too many layers of shingles can be the reason for walls that have cracked from moving away from the structure.

- The tower: If the tower was a later addition or overloaded with a heavier bell, it may be unstable, with a foundation that is slipping or pushing against the rest of the sanctuary.

- The attic: Look for stains, leaks, rot, termite-infested sagging beams and rafters, crooked or crumbling chimneys, and lack of insulation. Inspecting the roof from inside the attic may reveal an entire list of faults: damaged shingles or chimneys, separations, flashing problems, bent ridges, rotten towers, unreliable supporting beams, water and termite damage, and so on.

- The foundation: Determine whether it is the original foundation or if it was replaced in part. Check to see if there is a uniform construction of a mixture of stone, brick, and cement. If the mortar of the building foundation is turning into a powder, or if its stones are falling into a heap of rubble, then the sagging of the church walls is due to that faulty condition. Or the foundation may be strong and sound, but a wooden sill infested with termites cannot hold a horizontal structural line any longer and it causes the walls to drop. If the foundation is covered from the outside, a trip to the basement or cellar may answer further questions.

- The basement: Crawl into the corners and tight spots and use a flashlight and long screwdrivers to poke the wood and the masonry to see if there is rot or crumbling. How dry is the inside of the basement? If there is a leak, what is the source? How are the floor and the ceiling? Are there signs of asbestos or other insulation? Does the basement require cosmetic or structural work? The basement also is the area for checking heating, plumbing, and electrical installations, an examination requiring a building inspector. The presence of water is most likely the result of a permanent leak within the structure. According to the most common rule of any dwelling, water must be kept away from the inside of the building, for it creates a chain of unexpected damages.

- The walls: Falling patches of stucco and plaster may indicate serious wall movement, a simple leak, or other faulty conditions hidden for too long. If you knock on the walls and hear hollow sounds and plaster falling, this indicates an irreversible detachment of the plaster or stucco from the walls.

- The balconies: Sagging balconies and their crooked columns indicate erosion to their supports, which usually go below the sanctuary floor. An inspection may reveal either a lack of foundation for the balcony or wood rot at various levels.

- The floors: Caved-in floors may indicate the same thing, if their supporting beams are too weak to hold the weight they bear.

All these warnings are unmistakable signs of building decay. How to solve these problems is described in the following chapters. As mentioned earlier, it is important that the Restoration Committee document their findings in the planning stage by taking photographs of the inside and outside of the church. Later on, these records will help the restoration project by supplying the restorers with original lines and colors of certain areas that may have vanished in the meantime.

After the preliminary inspections are done and the problems identified, the church committee must answer some questions:

- Is there enough money to do the entire restoration at one time, even closing the church for that period? Or should restoration projects be scheduled over a number of years? What are the priorities?

- How much longer can restoration be postponed before the entire building is beyond repair?

- What time of year is the best for the work? Perhaps during winter is best, when contractors lack work and might work for less money. Will a heated tent over the outside working area make practical sense?

- Is the building structure in good shape, including the roof, the foundation, the tower, and the balconies? How about the floors and ceiling?

- Is the crack in the wall due to building settlement or is it a clear sign of a collapsing structure? Did anyone keep a written record of how a crack evolved over the past few years?

- Are the roof and/or clapboards/shingles due for replacement?

- Is it better to replaster or replace with drywall?

- What original parts or details are missing from the building? How can they be re-created? These might include tower railings, balusters, column bases and capitals, ceiling plaster of floral designs and moldings, etc.

- What original parts have been covered by later "improvements" and how could they be revived with minimum damage?

- ❧ Which "fake" details or later additions must be eliminated? These might include plastic shutters, siding covering the original lines, steps of chimney made of concrete blocks, and removal of every "creative chaos" accumulated over the years.

- ❧ Are the "boxed-in" beams acceptable or not?

- ❧ Should clear wood be used? Clear finish, stain, or paint?

- ❧ Should the window pulleys be repaired or the entire windows replaced?

- ❧ Should the old floor planks be fixed or replaced with a modern floor?

- ❧ Should a leak be fixed or should the entire area around the leak be redone?

- ❧ Should the old paint be stripped? Should it be sandblasted or sanded?

- ❧ How can the warm, inviting colors of the past be replaced with lead-free colors? Is a lesser quality paint all right to use?

- ❧ Is paint or stain better to use? What about oil, latex, or flat paint? One or two colors?

- ❧ Should the church be modernized with forced air heat and air conditioning?

- ❧ How many changes can the church take before losing its authentic look?

The list of questions and decisions is of course much longer, even up to deciding where to place the metal holder for the flag and other similar details that not too many people paid attention to before. Somehow, the planners usually come to the same conclusion: "They don't build like that anymore!"

For the duration of the restoration, the committee members will guide the project, but be prepared for some members to get tired of the project or choose to play a secondary role. The important roles of the Restoration Committee are to identify the scope of work required and a budget to cover that work, to hire a contractor, and to supervise or coordinate the restoration process.

Before I move on, let's not forget the landscaping, which, while not part of the restoration itself, does contribute to the church setting. The Restoration Committee will also be held responsible for protecting the plants, bushes, and trees around the church, some of them perhaps virtually irreplaceable. If the landscape is damaged by the contractor, tough negotiations are certain to follow.

There is one more subject often overlooked by the church committee: the church valuables. These may be weathervanes, stained glass windows, paintings, statues, pulpits, and other woodwork, neglected mosaic floors, covered inscriptions, plaques, and so on. Considering that a restoration project lasts longer than a year, a list of these valuables must be made and some of the items should probably be put into safes during the restoration.

I have had a few memorable experiences with valuables neglected by a church. Years ago, I was involved in restoring a meeting house in Fairfield County, Connecticut. I was told to have my workers take the weathervane down from the top of the steeple and to look for a place to gold-leaf it. The weathervane was a rooster made of hammered copper, and it was filled with holes. Older locals recalled a story that in 1776, British invaders aimed at the rooster with their muskets for target practice. Indeed, as the rooster came down, we heard things rolling noisily inside of it.

I brought the rooster home and for days it laid in front of my porch while I made calls to find a goldsmith. Finally I put the rooster in my car and drove to where I thought a shop was located. Unable to find it, I pulled into a parking space and looked for someone to give me directions. A gentleman sporting a well-trimmed beard got out of his car, took a look at the rooster in my back seat and, instead of answering my question about where the shop was located, asked:

"What do you want to do with the rooster?"

"I'm looking for a place to gold-leaf it."

"How much are you asking for the rooster?"

"The rooster is not for sale."

"You can make a very easy $40,000!"

"It is not my rooster. I need to take it back to the owner."

"I'll make a reproduction. I'll gild it and no one will know the difference."

"Forget about it!"

"Okay, I'll double my offer: $80,000. Let me have it."

"I just cannot do that!"

"I am an art dealer and I'll tell you what I'll do: we will put the rooster in an auction and we'll split the sale."

"I have to go!" and I left the parking space—not to look for the goldsmith shop, but to go straight back to the church. Suddenly the beaten-up rooster was too much responsibility for me to handle!

I called and told the story to the committee chairman. I returned the rooster to him, and it was promptly deposited in a local bank safe and appraised later at $240,000. Its value was more than the entire cost of restoring the church. The discovery made the news, and today the rooster gleams on top of the steeple, showing the way the wind blows. Many yards away, in the middle of the street island, waves a huge American flag, facing the rooster and its history.

Another time, I was working inside a small church, almost surrounded by a cemetery. One day I took a look at the tombstones and discovered a structure of some sort made from a few round, dirty pieces of stone. I asked my workers to take a look, to remove debris and see what might be there. After the priest asked us to wash it, it turned out to be a white marble baptismal of priceless design, inscribed with the church history. The piece was promptly reinstated in front of the altar. To this day, no one has figured out why it had been laid to rest in the cemetery's wild bushes.

In another instance, my painters discovered a wall inscription that had been papered over. The beautiful mural beneath the paper was restored, and today it adorns the inside of the church. Not only do the regular churchgoers enjoy it, it is now a tourist attraction as well.

One church tower was overloaded with a large bell that had replaced the original bell. The new bell was so heavy that the tower had begun to lean. Now the new bell was cracked, and we were asked to take it down. An electric chime was installed instead in the belfry. The priest and the committee members disputed what to do with the seemingly useless cracked bell. Because it was marked and dated, it looked like a museum piece. But the town did not have a museum, and neither the town hall nor the library could shelter the bell. Instead of selling it for scrap, the bell was eventually installed in front of the church. It "hangs" from its original wood beam while supported by a cement platform covered by a pointed wooden roof—a part of the church's history. Whether it is worth a lot of money or not, the bell has become a spiritual monument that serves as a much-loved backdrop for photos of weddings, baptisms, and visitors to the town.

No church should ever throw away its outdated bell if it cannot be left in its original place. Each bell is unique and personalized for the particular church, many times with historical information and design and beautiful lettering.

From the preceding example, one can easily conclude that in any restoration process something extremely valuable can be destroyed or discovered and returned to its full glory. That is why church representatives must always inspect the job site and be alerted to any curious signs of the past.

The restoration workers cannot be trusted with archaeological tasks. One never knows how many treasures have been lost because unknowing workers demolished them, threw them away, or covered them with plaster or sheetrock.

4

R A I S I N G   M O N E Y

Over the years, church members often notice the need for church repairs, and they may have discussed restoration ideas before and after the church service. Therefore, when the need for money arises for a restoration budget, people are not surprised, and they are often very cooperative.

Collecting money for any cause involves a strategic campaign, appealing both to the business and emotional sides of potential donors. Some parishioners may believe that quick repairs are sufficient for stopping a leak or preventing an area from collapse. No one will disagree that any delay or expense must be made to keep the church committee from eliminating injury and fire hazards, however. Falling plaster, ceilings, and chimneys, broken steps or floors, and electrical shorts must be attended to immediately in order to prevent personal injuries or the threat of fire.

But to engage the parish in a major restoration is a different story. Fund-raisers must explain that a settled crack or "map crackings" are much less troublesome than tension cracks or compression failures of the structure. As good and necessary as they are, repairs can be very expensive, and they may damage the building in the long run. Roof cement applied around the chimneys, on the slates or wood, is one example of the innocent "vandalism" produced by a contractor who does not understand church restoration. A major restoration may incorporate all these repairs into a better planned project, producing a like-new church that in the years to come will double or triple in value.

To eliminate any confusions or suspicions about how the money will be spent, the church Restoration Committee must put together a master plan. Like any other plan, this will help with the scheduling of work and eliminate costly changes. Furthermore, when people donate money they want to see a plan they understand—so the master plan must be written in layman's language with clearly laid-out solutions. A typical master plan should be divided into these sections:

- Roof

- Foundation

- Exterior Restorations

- Interior Restorations

Roof restoration includes repairs or the complete replacement of the roof, along with the flashings, gutters, downspouts, and vents. All such restorations must be done at the same time since flashings cannot be replaced a year after the reroofing is finished. Work in the attic can be attached to the roof project, especially if the roof is removed.

Foundation work is basically masonry jobs intended to stabilize the building and keep water from entering it.

Exterior restoration is the most frequently performed and consists of all structural repairs and painting. It includes energy-saving operations, such as insulation, and also the repair of old windows, installing storm windows, and similar work. Painting old siding or woodwork that is in bad shape may require stripping, which may be more expensive than replacing all the existing wood with new wood, and then finishing the job with fresh paint. Interior work is difficult to plan and carry out, especially if the church continues to be used during the restoration. All jobs have to be scheduled in stages with a logical order. Interior demolitions are very messy and any plumbing and electrical work must follow immediately. Wall and ceiling work must be done before finishing floors or furniture. Protection of church objects, especially the organ, and constant clean-up must be a preoccupation of the committee members.

Any new improvements must not ruin old ones. Durability, cost effectiveness, and beauty are the key words of any restoration work.

❧

Church donations are probably the best barometer of how the national economy is doing. When times are good, donations pour in; when people lose their jobs and their homes, donations stop. For this reason, church restorations tend to happen only periodically and in accord with people's prosperity and their subsequent generosity.

In some impoverished communities, churches are in poor physical condition all the time. Ironically, these distressed communities may harbor churches of unparalleled hidden beauty and faded grandeur, now almost in ruins. The congregations of these glorious but financially poor and dilapidated churches are happy if they can fix a leak in the roof or replace a broken pane of glass in the window.

Sometimes unexpected funds are provided. They may come from state or corporate donations, through the bequest of a deceased parishioner, or because someone just wants to help.

I recall a very large restoration project that would require the parish to solicit collections for many years before they could even begin the work. Meanwhile, rain dripped through the church ceiling during services, and the peeling paint no longer protected the exterior of the building. Unexpectedly, a devoted parishioner passed away and left the church a large sum of money—enough, in fact, to pay for the entire restoration, which was then able to start immediately.

An earthquake damaged the church in which I was baptized in Romania. I was visiting my family there, saw the church, and learned that it desperately needed funds to pay for materials and professionals to complete the repairs. Being so familiar with the church collection process and taking advantage of the strong American dollar, I was happy to be able to donate the rest of the money they needed to complete the work.

A typical fund-raising program begins with making people aware of what is wrong with the church structure and what has to be done. A professionally written letter addressed to the parishioners should describe the restoration plan and outline the amount of money needed to finance it.

Because a picture is worth a thousand words, it is worthwhile to display photographs showing the church's damages in the social hall. A tour of the affected areas should be arranged, and a well-versed member of the Restoration Committee might give a lecture explaining what is needed and why. An article in the local newspaper will also help by making people in the general community aware of the church's needs. The church bulletin should also keep every church member informed. A social event such as a party may be worthwhile to launch the fund-raising program.

Most people agree that it is essential to make the building structure sound and to replace the shattered roof, falling plaster, rotten woodwork, and peeling paint. But some people may strongly object to what they do not see as necessary: the addition of insulation, an elevator, air-conditioning system, alarm or sound system, and the like. To them, these are costly and unnecessary—the church didn't have them before and doesn't need them now. The church Restoration Committee must be ready to answer this type of response, with facts and figures supporting the need for change.

A good incentive for donations is their tax-free nature, and some well-to-do parishioners may be happy to have that deduction. Those who are not in a position to think about the benefit of deductions, though, will also do their best to pledge the most money they can spare. Typically, the church committee succeeds in raising most of the funds from regular parishioners, and the rest is donated by a generous benefactor or philanthropist, either outright or through matching funds.

Sometimes a restoration is so urgent that it cannot wait for donations—for example, the building is on the verge of collapsing. After the church is covered in blue tarps and walls are taken down, donations invariably follow!

There is a potential problem that the Restoration Committee must try to avoid, however: having hidden damages that require additional funds. When unexpected problems are found, it is much more difficult to convince the parishioners of the necessity for more donations. Avoid compromising the quality of the supplies and the quality of the work because the budget must be made to fit even unanticipated additional expenses.

Instead, my strong recommendation is to have the restoration budget be based on the winning bid—plus at least 15 percent that is set aside and reserved for unforeseen expenses.

❁

Obtaining a detailed written labor description is extremely important because it gives the bidding contractors the best opportunity for "comparing apples to apples." Price comparison is impossible without a precise description of the scope of the work. This detailed work list is *not a contract*. It is, however, an important piece of information that should be attached to any bid papers, along with blueprints, the contract, or a letter of agreement.

5

CHOOSING THE RIGHT
GENERAL CONTRACTOR

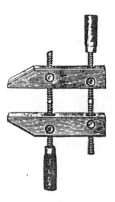

A typical general contractor hesitates to work on an old house. So many things may go wrong, and the contractor will end up underpaid. When it comes to a church restoration, the same contractors will think twice about doing it: too many "antique lovers" will expect a miracle to be performed on the dilapidated structure.

The site of the restoration area will be like a fishbowl in the middle of town for all to stop and comment about the work being done. A church essentially has thousands of owners. In addition, town inspectors and officials will be there all the time; they often work across the street from the church. Simply put, the responsibility is too huge for a handyman with just a truck and helper, or for a small contractor.

However, any church has among its parishioners a few builders or general contractors eager to prove themselves. For financial reasons they want the project very badly: the profit margin is plentiful, the job will keep their crew occupied for a long period of time, and their prestige will be greatly enhanced. One of them may be almost sure he or she will get the contract because of a personal connection to the priest/pastor, the committee members, and the budget.

So, this particular contractor is very optimistic and ready to do the work and will wine and dine the key church members while they are making a decision.

At this point, the Restoration Committee must be extremely careful in making a decision. Simply by consulting members of other churches that have already completed a restoration, they may find out that using an "in-house" contractor may just not be a good idea. To the contrary, it is like doing business with family members, which many times doesn't work out as envisioned.

First of all, choosing a particular contractor out of many who attend the church creates a general resentment among parishioners, especially among the "hurt" contractors. This sour feeling often generates ugly gossip and even nastier fights among different "partisan groups."

Second, none of the church contractors may be right for the job, for a church restoration is a highly specialized work requiring previous specific experience and craftsmanship. As a rule, a builder builds everything new, and a general contractor is most likely to work on patch-up jobs, or to be specialized in a particular line of work.

Many sour experiences have demonstrated over and over that a "privileged" contractor who starts the job with great fanfare and unmatchable confidence soon will conflict with his fellow churchgoers from the committee.

As in any other job, there is an endless list of what may go wrong during the restoration. Certainly, a church restoration has its own full list, and the hired workers will not be able to avoid testing it. Most of the time it is not their fault; it is just the nature of such complicated and delicate work. Yet, when a plan is executed in a reverse order or a blueprint is modified for practical reasons, a volatile situation becomes a major crisis. The main character in the unfolding drama is the contractor, who usually refuses to admit being wrong and will defend both the work crew and the company pride. But the committee member in charge of supervising the work, usually another contractor, has his or her own pride and power. Thus it becomes a no-win situation.

Another typical unpleasant situation happens when the contractor estimates a portion of the job but, for reasons not fully explained to the committee, later asks for more money to finish it. Or the contractor overcharges for "extras," already estimated much lower by the Restoration Committee.

Many of these incidents are solved in an amicable way to the benefit of the church, although sometimes a professional confrontation or a clash of egos results: the contractor refuses to cooperate, stops working, and seeks "justice." Or the contractor will quit before being fired from the job—and will leave the church for good.

It is not uncommon for an "in-house" architect, project manager, interior decorator, and other people involved in the restoration process to end up with the same sad experience. When this happens, who loses? The church does. It is now desperate to find a replacement and continue the work, while having to pay more to correct mistakes. Alas, bad things do not stop here. At this point, the parishioners are already divided in deciding who is right and wrong in the whole complicated restoration matter. Obviously some angry Restoration Committee members may leave the church as well, followed by their supporters.

In light of this nightmarish scenario (described at only a fraction of its real proportion), how does a church best choose a restoration contractor?

The answer is not simple, and it deserves mature and professional planning. First, no fewer than three contractors must be invited to see the job, read the documentation provided, and be encouraged to comment and ask questions. They should make an evaluation with their findings and describe the way they intend to carry out the restoration.

A good, free evaluation begins with a detailed general description of what struck the contractor the most. A true professional contractor or contractor's agent/manager may go to the library or will document in other ways knowledge about the church's past. The contractor will give professional impressions after having inspected the outside and the inside of the church, and then will show the way he or she believes the job must be done. The manner in which the contractor separates different areas and jobs tells a great deal about that person's level of skill and experience. In fact, this evaluation is more like the contractor's selling tool to the committee to help seal the deal. Any reputable contractor will not charge for an evaluation, which is more like an extended hand to show a willingness to do the job.

For the Restoration Committee this evaluation is an important document for putting together a sound bid.

It is most likely that an architect or an engineer will write the bid content, but no one can replace a contractor's keen eye for certain details. That perception is focused on what realistically needs to be done and how it should be performed. A contractor's building inspection will provide many important details that may escape someone who works in an office, regardless of title or experience.

It is only fair not to ask the contractor to give an estimate. Unfortunately, some committees will take advantage of a good and honest contractor to squeeze out the most information, including the price and scope of the work, and then they will hire a favorite contractor who did not jump through the same hurdles. This kind of nepotism always hurts the church and does no justice to the restoration industry.

The three prospective contractors must be local people within a comfortable driving distance from the church. This detail is vital, because their references and reputation are then easy to verify. Usually their crew is also made up of local people with local pride. Their short travel from home to church is a plus, especially in winter conditions or if traffic becomes an issue. A well-rested worker is a productive one. A fifty-mile radius is a good distance to consider as a fair travel limit.

If the contractors are recommended by someone, it is a good idea to check with the Better Business Bureau and talk to previous employers about their job performances and personalities. Inspect similar church restorations each contractor has done. Any serious contractor will do anything to get the job, even working for free in the beginning. Determining if a contractor works for free and determining the scope of that work is the invaluable role of the agent/manager, who can evaluate and negotiate these kinds of "favors."

The main questions remain: should the church hire one or more contractors? A big or a small contractor? An easygoing or a strict one? A contractor with a tie and Mercedes, or one dressed in a tank top and driving a beat-up truck?

The answer lies in the cost estimate, reputation, references, and the number of churches the contractor has successfully restored. There is nothing wrong with dealing with a "hungry" contractor, for such as person will do anything to prove reliable and skillful in restoration. Do not hire a contractor based solely on availability.

If the church committee is ready to handle more than one contractor (a carpenter, mason, roofer, painter, mechanic, electrician, and so on), then the Restoration Committee must coordinate their timing and keep everyone on the right job and schedule. They will need to make certain that none of the contractors backtracks on another's work. One general contractor who subcontracts different parts of the work is most likely a better choice for the Restoration Committee: the fewer people who share the responsibility, the better it is for the church.

All the qualified contractors should be invited to bid for the same job, and their sealed estimates must be opened at the same date and hour in front of the church committee, so everyone sees them at the same time.

A "request for quotation" may be the right way to let the contractors know how the church intends to pay for the work. This document simply states that sealed proposals are invited for certain work or equipment as described in the accompanying bid documents. Estimates shall be signed by a principal of the proposing firm and delivered not later than a specified date and hour. The committee reserves the right to reject any bid and award the job in the best interest of the church. The church may require the successful bidder to provide a 100 percent performance bond issued by a surety company licensed in the state. Should the bidder find any discrepancies or omissions therein, or be in doubt as to the meaning of any part thereof, that bidder should address the committee before writing the bid. All clarifications will be issued in the form of an addendum. No other advice shall be considered to modify the bid document.

Comparing written estimates in hiring the right person for the job may be essential because the lowest cost is not always the best choice. A low bid may also mean poor workmanship, cheap materials, cut corners—and room for later loopholes asking for "extras." Or it could be just a mistake in calculating the bid.

The committee must beware both a contractor who promises anything they dream of or one who asks too many questions and puts in too many conditions. In all these instances, the contractor is demonstrating one thing: he or she has only a vague idea of the complicated job awaiting him or her.

If the contractor is an immigrant who speaks little English and may have a problem understanding directions, things are different. An accurate translator is a big plus. As in any other field, an immigrant is often willing to work extra hard to please potential customers, will probably never play the prima donna role after being hired, and may consider finishing the job on excellent terms to be the biggest reward.

A good contractor:

- is a pillar of the community
- has a normal personal and family life (not in turmoil)
- is not a heavy drinker or a gambler
- is in good health
- is a person of integrity and is punctual
- radiates confidence and knowledge
- is honest and straightforward
- does not lose his or her temper

- ✴ takes orders well
- ✴ is flexible in listening to suggestions
- ✴ will admit mistakes and is eager to correct them at no extra cost
- ✴ is a doer, not a complainer
- ✴ does not gossip or blame others
- ✴ has a professional work crew
- ✴ takes full responsibility for the crew
- ✴ has tools that are well-kept and neatly stashed and vehicles that show no signs of accidents or neglect
- ✴ knows how to match old and new wood, plaster, stucco, and paint
- ✴ owns the scaffoldings, mortar mixer, and other heavy equipment

Indeed, a good contractor can be judged by the tools owned: wrecking bars; sledgehammers; circular saws; a carpenter's table; various drills; tool boxes with carpentry, masonry, mechanical, and painting kits; a large collection of rechargeable power tools to be carried on the scaffoldings; and other tools, including a vacuum cleaner. The bottom line is how the contractor deals with the church members and their reciprocal chemistry in planning and working together. How the Restoration Committee will address job-related actions and problems, and how the contractor reacts to the job demands will determine how much money and effort will be saved for all of them.

It bears repeating: never involve the priest/pastor, even as a referee for choosing who is right or wrong in a dispute. That role is spiritual, and a priest's or pastor's limited knowledge of construction is likely to allow regrettable blunders. The Restoration Committee must learn to trust retired engineers, building inspectors, and other businesspeople who have some experience in making restoration decisions.

One of the most overlooked issues is how to understand the contractor. It is well known that any general contractor works under tremendous pressure. After all, this is an individual who may have little formal education but certainly does have immense practical knowledge and pride in doing a complicated job. Contractors are aware that their best quality is to take directions well and do everything they can to do a good job. And they try hard to do work competently and well. But remember that they are in business to make a profit; otherwise they cannot continue to operate.

Contractors live and work under tremendous pressure from many sources: they must bid for jobs, negotiate deals, sign contracts, provide insurance papers and other legal documents, hire and schedule the right crews, assign and supervise work, pay workers on time, buy and bring materials, meet deadlines, observe OSHA and other safety rules, enforce these rules, provide first aid, meet with church representatives and inspectors, and explain any change of plans. All contractors havs a wide and expensive range of inventory, from powerful trucks and tools to ordinary hammers, pliers, and boxes of nails and screws. They must make sure everything works properly and that each of their workers is an ambulant workshop, equipped with everything needed to be effective on the job. Any delay because of missing or malfunctioning tools is lost time and costs the contracting company money.

Because so many things can go wrong with no warning, the contractor is constantly alert to prevent mistakes, accidents, and conflicts on the job. Such an individual may possess great working skills, but if not well organized and if not a "people person" it will be hard to please the church committee. Once again, the contractor's agent/manager can play an important role in making negotiations smoother and facilitating communication between all the parties involved in the restoration.

Therefore, the church committee does well to help make a contractor's life and job easier. This help starts by providing the "charitable and religious organizations exemptions certificate" that absolves the contractor from paying taxes for materials during the restoration work.

If some of the church members are on friendly terms with the "people from town hall," it is a good idea to introduce the contractor to them. Better yet, the same members should obtain permits and other approvals in the name of the church, so the contractor will not be entangled with bureaucratic delays. It is better for the contractor to stay on the job, rather than be lost in town hall corridors.

As the first one on the job and the last to leave, the contractor is aware of the slightest benevolent or unfriendly attitude. In other words, the church should cooperate with and meet the contractor halfway. If the committee can try to "walk in the contractor's shoes," most contractors will not want to take advantage of the situation. In fact, most will want to work even harder in order to reciprocate the trust and kindness. The church can help by giving the contractor easy access to the inside and outside of the building; assigning convenient spaces for parking, a dumpster, the scaffoldings, tool storage; designating a place to wash, somewhere to eat, and bathroom facilities; providing access to running water and electrical outlets; and offering other such "gratuities" that will be fully appreciated by the contractor and crew.

One of the jobs the contractor must be helped with is the protection of the church organ and any other similar sensitive but immovable instruments or valuable furniture. During the restoration process, the organ master should supervise the wrapping of the organ in a proper way, so that dust will not damage the instrument. Better yet, the church should do that job to avoid any possible inadvertent damages.

All this well-intentioned attitude does not mean the contractor and workers may walk into the church office any time they feel like it to ask for coffee or food, tell their stories, and feel too at home. If the restoration crew is larger than a few workers, the contractor should rent a portable bathroom for them. Their trucks and generators should not run without a reason, especially in front of the main entrances.

A decent dress code, regardless of how hot it is outside, must be demanded of all workers, known for their casual regard of clothing. Clean workers are better workers. With no exception, the contractor must enforce a minimum code of manners. Workers should refrain from cursing or using vulgar language, and shouting and indecent gestures should not be permitted. Smoking must be banned on the job because a cigarette butt thrown into a pile of dry wood can start a fire hours later, even in the middle of the night. Any competent contractor knows that a smoking worker is less productive than a nonsmoking one.

The committee members must supervise the way the workers handle their materials during and after the work. At one church, the painters folded their drop cloths and simply put them under the sanctuary window, beneath a bush hedge. Hours later, after nightfall, a fire erupted on that spot. The firemen came in time to extinguish the flames that nearly engulfed the large stained-glass window. Only the wood around the window was damaged, and the stone foundation was stained with suds. The windows were fixed later by the contractor at no additional charge. The fire was ignited by the drop cloths, of course—they were soaked with paint and paint thinner and dumped on top of a floodlight that was hidden in the bushes. The sensor light turned on when covered by the cloths (darkness), and the heated bulb set the drop cloths afire.

Because the church is a special institution with a sacred mission, the crew will often have to stop work during religious services, weddings, funerals, holidays, celebrations, and other such events. So it is particularly important to keep the job site clean and neat for the church to function properly. To respect church privacy is extremely important as it represents so many people. I recommend having a tactful church representative deal with the contractor or agent/manager, not with the workers. Workers take orders from their direct employer.

And please refrain from ever asking the contractor how many hours it will take to do a job, how much workers are paid, and any other inappropriate questions! Always remember that a restoration contractor is not a handyman with a truck, so expenses are complex and difficult to explain to a person outside the trade. In general, labor cost is usually three times the cost of materials. To this is added the cost of scaffoldings, operational costs, insurances, overhead and profit costs, and so on. All in all, a successful self-employed contractor is a capable entrepreneur. Just to stay in business is a performance in itself. Therefore, please show respect for the contractor's personality and work.

Another piece of advice I give to Restoration Committees is: never choose the church janitor or the custodian to represent the church to the contractor. Many of these people do fix-it jobs themselves, many with great working skills, but they are not contractors. For some reason, having custodians and contractors discuss construction is like setting gas on fire: their egos clash and sooner or later the situation erupts. As I have stated before, the best person to deal with a contractor is a church member with a proven reputation and at least some knowledge of the construction business.

Always address the problem and how to solve it, rather than looking to blame someone. Leave the lines of communication open both ways between the church and the contractor. Both sides need to cooperate.

Once the contractor has been selected, the committee must keep a file of all the restoration documents, correspondence, and papers that relate to the activities of the contractor, architect, and inspectors, as well as reports of each important meeting, and so on. All money-matter papers (estimates, bids, contracts, change of work orders, and letters of agreement) must be in writing and legally enforceable. In case of litigation, the church must be able to document its case in court. Luckily, this is a very rare occurrence!

6

W R I T I N G   T H E   C O N T R A C T

There are standard contracts that one can buy from stationery stores, download from the Internet, or request from architects. One of them is the AIA (American Institute of Architects) Document A107-1997, which is an abbreviated Standard Form of Agreement Between Owner and Contractor for Construction Projects, approved and endorsed by the Associated General Contractors of America. It spells out the essential parts of any legally enforceable contract, and most institutions successfully use this.

Most printed contracts are lengthy, full of intricate details needed in case of a lawsuit, and cover everything regarding the work to be done. The only problem is that not too many contractors bother to read them. All too often, neither do the members of the Restoration Committee. Both sides know too well that if something goes terribly wrong with the restoration, the entire well-written contract is not worth the paper it is written on.

For that good reason, most restoration contracts are "homemade" —tailored by people who know the construction trade. In plain and explicit language these contracts spell out exactly what and how things must be done and under what conditions.

A contract should include the following:

- ☙ The location of the church

- ☙ The names of those signing the contract and their responsibilities

- ☙ A brief description of what kind of work has to be done

- ☙ General requirements, clearly stated, about who is going to supply the labor, materials, tools, scaffoldings, and other equipment

- ☙ A detailed description of the scope of the work, outlined in well-defined areas, including specific jobs to be done. Certain restrictions can be included here, such as "do not paint over dirt, rust, scale, grease, moisture, scuffed surfaces, etc."

- ☙ How to protect the work from natural elements and negligence

- ☙ Work to be excluded (note: it is common for the contractor to include some small free-of-charge jobs)

- ☙ Provisions for "changing the order," which entitle the contractor to do extra jobs and ask for more money

- ☙ Conditions that include what the owner and contractor must provide and be aware of; a list of contractor's insurances and liabilities; the use of space and facilities; who will do the daily and final cleaning; how to coordinate work; the names of the representatives; the need for a waiver of lien from all people paid by the contractor; who will obtain necessary permits; and proof of the manufacturer's label and instructions for specific materials to be used

- ☙ A schedule of work, showing the starting and completion dates as well as job priorities and deadlines for various stages of the work. It is common for the Restoration Committee to stipulate that the work will start within a number of days from the signing of the contract and that it will be completed in a certain number of days (or "working days"). If the work is done outside, a working day is usually a day of good weather. If the job is supposed to be completed in thirty working days, but the weather is bad for ten days and another three days are national or religious holidays, then the job will last forty-three days from start to finish, with no fault on the contractor's side.

- ❧ Cost and terms of payment, specifying the total sum of money for the work, is divided according to a reasonable schedule. It is only fair for the contractor to ask for a 1 percent deposit to save the awarded job in his schedule, and to ask another 9 percent when he starts working. It is not recommended for the church to make weekly payments, because limited work may be done in poor weather if the job is to be performed outside. It is better if the entire restoration is divided into stages, with precise payments to be made when each stage is completed. Or you might simply divide the entire work into a few clear parts of work completed, such as when the work is one-quarter completed, one-third completed, half completed, and the work has passed inspection.

- ❧ Safety and environmental issues

- ❧ Dates of final inspections

- ❧ Warrantees and guarantees of work and materials

- ❧ Consequences for failure to perform work and failure to pay the contractor

- ❧ Termination of contract specifying the failure of the contractor to perform the job according to the Restoration Committee's expectations

- ❧ Guarantees and warrantees for the work done

- ❧ Signatures and dates to seal the contract

- ❧ Addendums (these may be added later) for extra work, change of work orders, and rescheduling of payments

It is fair for the Restoration Committee to ask the contractor to keep the same crew on the job, or to change workers who may not perform well. Any other important points may be included as well. Sometimes the church sends a Proposed Contract to the contractor who must send back a Letter of Agreement, in which the contractor agrees or disagrees with the terms laid out in the Proposed Contract. I repeat: safety and quality of work must be key stipulations in whatever contract is ultimately drawn up.

❀

Another important duty for the church Restoration Committee is to share the job order with the contractor, or to coordinate all the contractors involved in the restoration project. Coordinating the flow of the jobs or contractors with their job schedule will cut costs, save time, avoid conflicts, and produce a successful result.

As I have noted, there are no standard recipes for how to conduct a restoration project because churches are different in style and they present endless job combinations. Addressing these issues logically will save headaches, materials, labor, and money, so a certain practical judgment must be observed. And again, it is important to determine what time of the year the restoration will take place and what areas will be involved. Organizing the correct order to the jobs involves determining whether or not each job is long- or short-term and prioritizing the jobs.

Let's pause to take a look at some of the areas a contractor will be concerned with. It will serve Restoration Committees well to understand these "rules" that are basic for construction and restoration work.

RULE ONE: Ensure Safety

Safety is crucial for any construction activity.

- ❧ Use scaffoldings following the strict OSHA rules: hard hat, harness, protective gear/clothes, etc.
- ❧ Always make the building watertight at the end of each working day, regardless of the weather forecast

- Plan an escape route in case of emergency
- Never drink alcohol on the job; illegal drugs are out of the question
- Provide a safe area for smokers, if there are workers who must smoke
- Identify a safe loading and unloading area for trucks, materials, dumpsters, etc.

RULE TWO: Prepare for Emergencies

These may involve temporary and fairly simple remedies, like fixing the gutters and downspouts in order to lead water away from a basement. Such work is not part of the restoration job, but it affects the building structure and makes the job of restoration easier later on. Let's say, for example, that rain is pouring into a church through a growing crack. The crack may signal a structural problem—it must be attended to before the wall, sitting on saturated ground, begins to crumble. A drainage system may need to be installed immediately as an "emergency" measure.

RULE THREE: Work in Logical Order

Consider the logical order of working areas. Obviously, any structural work has top priority because it improves the safety of the building and prevents accidents. Collapsing walls and floors infested with termites might also be at the top of the list. If the foundation crumbles under the weight of the building, or stones and bricks are pushed out of alignment, that is a logical area to address early on because it will provide a stronger base for work done subsequently either inside or outside of the church.

RULE FOUR: Avoid Backtracking

Electrical work must be done before painting, and floors must be sanded after painting. The roof structure must be fixed before covering the church with a new layer of shingles.

RULE FIVE: Coordinate Effort

Coordinate the various jobs that can be done simultaneously, ensuring that each job complements the others. Many jobs can go on at the same time, but each one must have its own "breathing space," especially if scaffoldings or heavy equipment are involved. As an example, the contractor can make full use of scaffoldings while they are in place. Fixing a weathervane is a minor job, with little expense, when the steeple is wrapped in scaffoldings for other reasons. On the other hand, fixing the weathervane by itself becomes an entire project, difficult to accomplish without erecting scaffolding. Another example is the installation of air conditioning ducts in the walls, along the walls, under the floor, on the floor, and so on, and new light fixtures in the ceiling, while stripping down the plaster walls. (See pictures 1 and 2.) A "naked" building structure is an ideal job site for any improvement or addition through its walls. Making the best use of space and time is good, solid restoration procedure.

Picture 1 (top) and 2 (above). While restoring plaster work with old-fashioned wood lath, do the electric and air conditioning work.

As a word of caution, I warn Restoration Committees not to trust the plumber or electrician to respect architectural values. They have different priorities, including their own safety rules. They will make sure their work passes technical inspection, but they are less likely to be concerned with preservation and restoration issues.

Again, the Restoration Committee members play an important role in keenly observing and watching over the work. They must be vigilant in mixing practicality with historical style and artistic taste, keen at detecting hidden faults, and never shy about asking the contractor to rectify them in time. An example of something that can be minor in appearance but huge in later consequences if it is not attended to is making sure that all heat and air conditioning ducts are free of debris, sawdust, cigarette butts, food, bottles, and cans. It is amazing to see how, even in new homes, excellent craftsmen often show gross negligence in keeping their job site clean. The contractor may not be the most careful person in that respect, either. It is up to the agent/manager and the Restoration Committee to inspect everything before areas are sealed.

In fact, church representatives must exercise common sense with any new initiative or measure so as to protect the beauty of the church without undermining its functionality. For example, fire extinguishers can be installed inside built-in compartments that blend with the church's furniture and its religious mood. Secular items that are necessary but difficult to conceal include the white-and-red exit signs and automatic sprinklers. These, too, can be treated aesthetically with frames or boxes that take little from the budget but make a difference between a well-planned restoration and a plain restoration.

Always remember: you can never do enough to protect and beautify an old church!

✠

7

RESTORATION AREAS AND THEIR SCOPES OF WORK

The American church is unique for combining masonry with woodwork, so as to have clapboard walls outside and plaster walls inside, all covered by a slate roof and resting on a stone foundation covered by stucco. Starting from the top, the jobs can be divided into distinct areas.

ROOF ELEMENTS

Dome

A church's dome can be seen in many shapes as a cupola, drum dome, sail dome, pendentive, domical, or parachute structure. Any work on the dome requires complicated scaffoldings and special protection of the covering metal or wood. Restoration may include patching the copper or wood cover, reinforcing its structure, and gold-leafing or painting the dome. Painting will never match expensive gold-leafing, but when done in bright colors, it can make an impressive visual impact.

Steeple

The steeple marks the height of the church. In America, most steeples are made of wood with some version of the needle spire, broach spire, or octagonal spire. Steeples are strongly built with oversized beams and usually shelter the bell room.

Tower

Traditionally built of stone or brick, the tower is a clear feature of the medieval castle or fortress bastion. The church keep, or square don-jon, goes to a certain height and still features arrow-slit windows and top-crenellated walls. Side church towers still keep their castle look with top bartizan, battlements, and a dwarf gallery. Because the tower roof is usually flat, railings have often replaced the crenellations. Later, the railings became a permanent fixture and an art form of upper woodwork around or on top of the belfry. Magnificent urns and other ornaments may mark the corners or the railing posts, usually made of wood.

In one restoration job, an initial scope of work for these upper church structures was written by a Restoration Committee because water leaks in the tower had begun to trickle into the sanctuary, and the church needed a painting job. The following general format was given to the contractor:

1. Erect scaffoldings to the top cross. Build a strong platform to protect the main roof from the weight of upper scaffolding.

2. Strip the paint from all wood areas above the soffits, including the railings, the urns, moldings, and panels.

3. Clean the remaining chemicals from the bare wood and let it "heal."

4. Fix damaged wood.

5. Hand sand, patch, and prepare bare wood for painting.

6. Touch up darkened spots with "kills."

7. Fix and caulk/waterproof all cracks.

8. Prime the wood, including the backs of unglued pieces.

9. Protect the environment and dispose of regular debris and lead paint/chemical waste in the proper landfill; provide the owners with the necessary certificates.

Because the church was almost three hundred feet high, this scope of work was conceived from the ground and mostly from an office. After the scaffoldings wrapped the entire church, everyone had a big surprise: the previous restoration of twenty years earlier had done more damage than good. Because those workers had used ladders or hung by ropes, they had done sloppy jobs. And the Restoration Committee had had no way of inspecting the work from the ground.

Taking advantage of the situation, the dishonest contractor and his workers cheated the church by doing marginal patching jobs in those difficult-to-access areas. Shortly after the restoration, the dome was leaking badly into the church. When the new workers reached the church top on the scaffolding, they discovered that the damaged drum under the dome had never been fixed. Previous workers had merely wrapped the dome in plastic wallpaper and painted over it. The rest of the wood was painted without primer.

From the street, the drum looked in perfect condition, but underneath the painted surface, almost all of the wood had begun to rot. Moreover, the copper flashings from above the crown moldings and soffit boards had not been changed and instead had been smeared with roofing cement and painted over. (See pictures 3 and 4.)

After the plastic cover (which trapped the moisture behind it) was removed, the entire disaster was revealed; the head board, vertical boards, skirt board, and crown moldings were mostly rotten. The beautiful ornate drapery from around the dome drum was barely holding in the rot, and it needed an extensive epoxy job to replace its missing spots. The belfry had to have all moldings around the raised panels replaced, as well as the crown moldings in the clock section.

Below the tower and around the main roof, things were even worse with the beautiful railings, their spindles, and boxes with urns

Picture 3 (top). A badly damaged roof corner. **Picture 4 (above).** *An example of a poor previous restoration where the workers covered holes with duct tape and painted over it.*

on top of them. Most of the wood was so far beyond repair that it had to be reproduced and replaced. The urns were fiber-glassed. New flashings were installed all over, wherever there was a flat surface and around the railing posts. Crown molding under the gable roof had to be removed and replaced, as did almost all panels and trim work. In a matter of days, the same restoration project tripled its initial scope of work and cost.

The lesson was clear: a church representative must always inspect the hard-to-reach areas during a restoration and make sure everything is done according to the signed contract. Nowadays, the whole project can be videotaped with close-ups that focus in on details and hidden spots to be double-checked.

Turrets

Mini-domes that enhance the large roof lines, turrets lead the eyes to the central tower or steeple. Highly ornate, they come in shapes —domed, imperial (the Russian onion shape), conical, and spiral. Any stone church or cathedral is most likely to have turrets on the roof corners, in the middle of the roof ridge, and around the steeple. These turrets look sharp and charming, but they can be dangerous when their bases do not hold them strongly enough.

A large and very tall stone church with a magnificent steeple had four turrets around its base. One stormy night, two of these turrets toppled through the roof into the sanctuary. One turret crashed in the middle of the organ pipes and continued its fall through the balcony. Its damages matched a cluster bomb's, and the splinters from the roof, plastered ceiling, and pipes were scattered everywhere. The other turret fell on the street, making a hole in the pavement. Thankfully, because the accident happened in the middle of the night, no one was walking below and no one was hurt. The lesson is simple: all those beautiful ornaments above the roof must be checked periodically for safety.

Steeples, towers, and turrets can be greatly affected by hurricanes, earthquakes, seismic stress, building settlement, and other causes that force them to lean or even move from their original vertical lines. It is important to inspect them and make sure they have an unbreakable line of support and resist torquing.

All these upper parts of the church carry lightning rods or Franklin rods, designed to conduct air electricity from the top of the building to the ground. In this way, the church is protected from lightning and fire. A lightning rod is made up of a rod with a point and a ball, and a wire conductor is made of copper or aluminum that ends with a ground rod. For obvious reasons, when working on the steeple, the contractor must temporarily remove the lightning rod. Because its cable lasts only some fifty years, the contractor may be asked to replace it. The entire system, however, must be upgraded in order to meet today's lightning protection code. A professional installer should be entrusted with this highly specialized job.

The lightning rods are usually part of the weathervane installation, which features the well-known hammered copper grasshoppers, roosters, horses, arrows, sailing boats, and other masterpieces created by blacksmiths. Because of the access scaffoldings provide to the top of the church, these expensive antique pieces are the most often-stolen church valuables.

Belfry

This is the room where the bell and the clock are located. It is also an area riddled with damages because it is usually an open room with intricate designs, mostly in wood, fully exposed to weather elements. It is a place only partially seen from the ground, and one difficult to reach and fix. The most commonly damaged part of the belfry is the floor, which also serves as a roof for the rest of the steeple or the tower. This roof is usually flat, with a hatch door and many flashings that never seem to stay in place. The scope of the work is similar to that needed for the upper church structure.

As briefly mentioned earlier, the tower or the steeple, especially if it was a later addition to the church, often can lose its verticality and cause damages to the rest of the building. Mainly, it may push against the bottom roof, which can create structural problems, signaled by serious wall cracks and jamming of the windows.

Such a case was corrected in one church by jacking the tower up to its initial position. The job consisted of using two steel beams inserted through the roof into the basement, where large cement footings were built to support the beams' lower ends. The beams were cut to reach the belfry level exactly where a strong platform was built for the beams to push against the tower, moving it into the vertical line. After the steel beams were in place, they were jacked up little by little, until the tower regained its correct position. Then the basement beam footing was raised to firmly keep the beams at the same correct height. The steel beams, which were slid along the narthex walls, were boxed in to look like wooden columns and painted to match the rest of interior. Miraculously, the roof and the building structure came right back and fit with the realigned tower. Minor gap lines were reflashed and covered to match the rest of the roof.

Roof

Most churches have gabled or hipped-gable pitched roofs that end with a steeple or various types of turrets. Regardless of its shape or structure, the roof is the first and main obstacle to keep water away from the building. Between water, high winds, heavy snow, and scorching sun, the roof takes the most abuse from nature. Waving and rippling roofs are the top priority job on the restoration list. It is only

Picture 5. *Roof damaged by a leak due to lack of proper metal flashings, cracks, and missing stucco.*

common sense to know that no other restoration jobs are possible if the roof is leaking or falling apart (see picture 5).

While inspecting the attic, one may notice that the outside light "peeps" through the roof lines and holes. If the roof is sagging, if the sky is visible through the roof, if there are water stains on the rafters or down on the attic floor, if there are any signs of water at all, there is no doubt that a new roof is needed immediately.

The Restoration Committee must decide whether to cover the church with modern roofing materials or with traditional ones. Modern materials include asphalt shingles, which are inexpensive and easy to install but lack the often-desired "old look" and may not have a long life. Traditional roofs are those made of slate, wooden shingles, clay (Spanish-style), and metal, or they may be made of ferrous metal coated with tin or zinc. Their overlapping structure and downward inclination forces water to roll off the building. Flat roofs are covered with roll roofing and hot tar. Built-up roofing lasts longer but it costs more and needs special drainages. This type holds and leads the water toward lower downspouts off the building.

In making their decision about the roof, the committee members should also know that most church roofs have one layer of original shingle wood, covered with two or three layers of asphalt shingle. The irony is that often the original roof still holds strong and seals the building better than the modern additions.

While the contractor removes the layers of the old roof, the committee must inspect its ridges, beams, purlins, rafters, studs, struts, and other lumber components for cracks, corners out of joint, rot, and insect infestation. This is the ideal time to rebuild the roof structure and jack it back into its original line before rebracing, reinforcing, or even reshingling a roof.

In choosing to re-
place a roof, the com-
mittee members face
a tough decision right
away; should they
leave the open sheath-
ing for a traditional
roof, or should they
cover it with plywood
for an asphalt-shingle
roof? (See picture 6.)
Plywood adds more
weight and, therefore,
the roof structure
must be reinforced.

Picture 6. *An old-fashioned wood shingle roof was covered by an asphalt shingle roof, but the planks underneath could not hold it any longer. To rebuild the roof, remove everything to the beams and rafters and apply plywood roof sheathing. Then cover with roofing felt before nailing a new asphalt shingle roof.*

Like any other compact sheathing, plywood provides a smooth surface that must be covered with building paper and an ice barrier.

A word of caution: an asbestos roof must be removed by a contractor certified in asbestos abatement. While asbestos proved to be
an unbeatable construction and insulation material for centuries,
today its use is prohibited by health and industry codes of safety.

Following is a condensed scope of roof work provided by a
Congregational Church in 1991:

For the sanctuary (Note: The sanctuary is a rather small area in
front of the altar. The main room of a church is the nave, divided by
aisles of pews. Yet the term "sanctuary" is often loosely used to describe the interior of the church. The narthex is the room between
the main entrance doors and the main body of the church.):

1. Supply and erect all necessary scaffoldings.

2. Remove all layers of old roofing material (one wood shingle
   layer and two asphalt layers). Also remove roof gutter straps,
   hangers, and gutters. Gutters are not to be cut, but left
   unsoldered. Gutters will be repaired by others.

3. Repair any minor defects in the old boards (underlying
   sheathing) if required.

4. Inspect all wood structures. Notify owner if replacement is required. This also applies to major defects in underlying sheathing.

5. Clean all exposed roof areas. Hammer all nails sticking out.

6. Install one layer of water-ice barrier (GAF "Weather Watch" or equal) for a width of three feet, starting at the eaves. The rest of the roof area is to get one layer of #30 felt cover.

7. Install a copper fascia drip around the perimeter of the sanctuary roof.

8. Install forty-year fiberglass shingles made by GAF under the trade name of "Timberline Ultra" over entire roof area. Color: "Weathered Wood Blend." On ridges, use GAF Timbertex shingles. Prior to installing ridge or hip shingles, contractor is to coordinate work with the Wood's Lighting Protection Co., which will install cables in the ridge.

9. Inspect flashings around church steeple structure. Advise owner if the flashing has to be repaired or replaced.

10. Check the existing valley (see picture 7). If it is determined that this is to be replaced, the cost of copper sheeting, installed, will be $x.xx per linear foot.

11. All nails shall be hot dipped and zinc coated, except for nails fastening any copper members. In this case, use copper nails.

The color, design, texture, durability, wind resistance, fire rating, and safety level of any roof must be determined by the owner and mentioned in the contract. The contractor may be asked to maintain the same undulated roof line as before, reinforcing and restoring the roof, for people were attached to its old look.

Ice barrier is now automatically included in any new roofing. Very rarely do churches have heating coils along the eaves so that ice dams will be immediately melted.

Flashings

Flashings, counter-flashings, and hip flashings are other main waterproof materials for the roof valleys, around the base of the steeple, chimneys, dormers, skylights, and other roof fixtures. Aluminum, galvanized steel, copper, and leaded copper are the most common. Copper will turn green over time and that color seems to fit any church.

The church committee must make sure that the same metal is used for joining because different metals produce an adverse chemical reaction and leaks will follow. The nails used must also be compatible. Make sure that the life span of the flashings matches that of the roof. Fifteen-year aluminum flashings are a poor choice for a thirty-year roof.

The roof lines must be cut perfectly along or around the flashings so water can run smoothly, without splashing under the shingles.

Picture 7. An outdated slate and asphalt shingled roof with a valley and flashings that are no longer waterproof. Roof flashings were sloppily added and then had to be patched to prevent leaks. Ultimately this old slate roof had to be completely replaced with an asphalt shingle roof that matched the colors, and new flashing and gutters had to be added.

Some churches may want to keep the original look of wooden shingles and wooden gutters, even with wooden downspouts. Much precise carpentry is involved and the committee members should hire a specialized contractor for such a job.

Slate and tile roofs are used less frequently today, and existing ones are rapidly being replaced with asphalt shingle roofing. To fix those vanishing roofs is not that difficult, but it is a dying art. It is important to protect the rest of the roof by laying "catwalks" of plywood from the ladder or scaffolding to the area in need of repairs. Walking back and forth on slates or tiles will damage such a delicate roof—which ironically is the most resistant over time.

The Restoration Committee members have a duty to minimize the mistakes that roof contractors might make despite their best intentions. One of these is to open too large an area for the reroofing. It is wiser to work on small areas, which are easy to cover in case of bad weather. Regardless of the forecast, at the end of each day the stripped roof must be waterproofed with tarps nailed with two-by-four-inch wood pieces and other ways to keep rain from entering the building. Tightening the tarps with only ropes is not enough to keep the winds from blowing the tarp off the roof.

Gutters

Usually made from the same materials as the flashings, gutters must match them, of course. The gutters can be painted, but only when they are dry and clean, and any copper cannot be painted. Old churches, especially rectory buildings, have roofs trimmed with "yankee gutters." Highly ornate and beautiful to admire, these wooden gutters have a major drawback: they bring rain inside the building and the downspouts go straight into the basement, often inside the walls.

Yankee gutters are wide and deep, and they function well for a long period of time, but the inevitable happens: they rot. They have a unique history of improvised fixes: lining with copper, coating with hot tar, plugging with cement, and performing many other desperate measures trying to stop a leak. What all these measures actually do is trap moisture between the covering and the wood, making things worse.

When asked to redo a yankee gutter, nine out of ten contractors will make the same recommendation: eliminate it, roof over it, and use regular gutters for the drippage line. Replacing a yankee gutter is a difficult and expensive job. If it is done properly, it may last fifty years without major problems. Never paint or coat the inside of the wood gutters, and use rubber caulking.

Gutters must be installed with a pitch for water, and they must be wider than the end of the roof in order to collect the water falling towards the downspouts. Providing wire strainers for the downspouts is a good idea, especially if they go into the ground pipes to exit in a dry well. Covering the gutter with a protective screen may cause more problems than it avoids. The cover may indeed cover the gutter with leaves, and the water will roll free on top of it.

Wood gutters should be painted outside, and only rubber caulking should be used. If possible, run a hose from the roof in the newly installed gutters to see how they work.

Where the roof water goes is another important issue for the church committee to discuss with the contractor. A city sewer is the ideal drainage, if available. If the water from the downspout is led by pipes into the ground, then a large opening farther down the hill must be available to collect and lead the water away.

Problems arise when the church is set on a flat land that is full of clay or saturated with water. Accumulated water is forced to go into the only area available: the basement. To correct this problem, more than one dry well must be dug away from the church. The larger the hole in the ground, the better the collection point for the water coming from the roof and the drainage. The dry well works on the septic tank system, except that the holes must be filled with large stones so the surface of the ground can safely bear weight. In-ground basement windows (windows that are partially below ground with a semicircular metal retaining wall) also use the dry well placed below the window base so water doesn't flood the window.

Cornice

This feature is probably the most distinctive church woodwork displayed under and around its roofs. It gives the building that unique and rich style, but it is a contractor's nightmare. Many carpentry, masonry, and painting jobs are involved to fix and restore a cornice, which always requires scaffolding.

The mason or carpenter must check and reinforce the wall that supports the cornice, often without disturbing it. Galvanized nails and screws must be used with care so as not to weaken the wall behind the cornice. Copper or lead-copper flashings have to be masterfully done to ensure the waterproofing and the aesthetic look of the cornice. Repairs are difficult, and often portions of rotten cornice have to be taken down for replacement. And to do so, a contractor must have a first-class carpenter.

The committee members must inspect the work and take pictures of these detailed restorations, and oversee the caulking, puttying, and priming operations, because once these jobs are finished, no one from the ground will ever know if the job was done correctly. What they will see is a rapid deterioration of the cornice badly restored by a contractor cutting corners.

Gables

Gables can be large, flat, and vertical portions of the roof structure that take a lot of beating from the elements. A plain gable is much easier to restore than a highly ornate "shaped" and "Dutch" gable. The presence of round, octagonal, and various other windows further complicates the job of carpenters and painters. Gables are neither real walls nor a roof, but they rot and crack more often than any other part of the church. For that reason, it is not unusual to have the gable fixed and painted more often than any other church area.

Columns

Columns are made for a dual and equal purpose: to support and enhance the exterior and interior of a church. They make a lasting impression with their ornate capitals, foliages, dentils, massive shafts, triglyphs (vertical lines), pedestals, and plinths, all imitating Greek and Roman temples.

Colonial churches seem to favor mostly fluted and octagonal wood columns, and just like the cornice, the columns add a look of eternity, glory, and majesty to any building. Money was clearly not a problem when these churches were constructed.

However strong they are, the columns must be well maintained before they become hard to salvage and beyond repair. Solid or hollow inside, when a column goes bad, it goes bad all the way, usually from the bottom up. The reasons for damage are common and easy to detect and prevent: water saturation, lack of ventilation, peeling paint, and too much exposure to sun and rain, for example. Some damage is less obvious. Drilling into the column at different levels may reveal surprising decay. Sometimes the column is held in place only by numerous coats of paint that have cemented it over the years. (See pictures 8 and 9.)

Picture 8 (left) and 9. *An example of before and after restoration showing how many things can go wrong with the base of a column: rotten, split, and missing wood, lead paint cemented, and rusted nails.*

Water damage can be stopped by installing proper flashings on all flat surfaces, which must be in perfect shape, and open vents (not larger than one inch) must be inserted on both column ends.

A scope of work for column restoration reads like this:

1. Erect scaffolding around the column.

2. Strip paint to bare wood, wash it, and let it "heal."

3. Properly dispose of lead paint and stripping chemicals.

4. Rebuild missing parts of capitals and crown moldings/foliage.

5. Replace rotten areas in main shaft.

6. Jack up and support column to rebuild each base.

7. Drill and install two-inch vents on top and bottom of columns.

8. Match all rebuilding to existing design and fabrication. Submit all other design changes for approval before work is started. All new wood is to be clear and of strong grain.

9. Predrill with holes all trim to be nailed, and cap with wood putty before painting over.

10. Sand by hand before each coat of paint.

Restoring a column is a big and time-consuming job to be done by a professional with a lot of experience. However, the following guidelines apply to any column restoration.

Any wood damage less than ten inches in diameter can be successfully plugged with nonshrinking wood consolidants and wood epoxy, which is often stronger than the original wood. It can be used for filling open joints and even reshaping parts of the missing moldings.

Most common column repairs are done with wood plugs. Larger damaged areas must be cut out, like stave sections, and replaced with similar wood, preferably glued and tightly clamped. Allow at least a week for the new wood to settle in, shave it to match the rest, sand it over, prime and paint.

The intricate work of making plaster or fiberglass moldings can be done by casting them, or you can have a specialist make wooden forms to reproduce details missing from the capitals (see pictures 10 and 11).

Picture 10 (left) and 11. An example of wood and paint restoration of cap/capital column with foliage, dentil work, and round siding. Notice the air vent placed at the top of the column to keep the inside ventilated and dry.

Most often, rotten wood bases and their rings can be replaced with cast iron ones. To jack up a column is a delicate job and must be done by people who know how to handle the many structural elements involved.

Erecting scaffolding is a job in itself. None of the preceding jobs can be done without it. The dictionary states that a scaffold is a raised platform for workers to sit or stand on, and scaffolding refers to a system of scaffolds. If in the past scaffolding meant using boards and lumber to help reach a high area, nowadays the notion of scaffolding is a complicated and precise way to ensure a safe place for workers.

Tubular segments with brackets, clamps, safety pins, and anchorage and footing points, secured with guardrails and personal fall arrest systems (harnesses, lifelines, D-rings, etc.), platforms, decks, and ladders provide a safe working environment. Since any scaffolding job automatically becomes a "hard hat area," Occupational Safety and Health Administration rules and regulations dictate measures to prevent accidents. (See picture 12.)

OSHA inspectors are attracted to the site of any scaffoldings like flies to honey. They have excellent ways of surveying and inspecting a construction site, and they allow no bending of the rules. Their repeated fines can put a contractor out of business in no time.

Church scaffoldings are both difficult and spectacular to erect. They are probably one of the most intricate and imaginative supports in the construction industry. With no two churches alike, there is no pattern for contractors to follow. A three-hundred-foot-high scaffolding with

Picture 12. *Modern scaffolding and the proper way to hoist materials to the top of it.*

many interruptions at different levels for gable roof, tower, railed platform, and dome offers a challenge for the contractor's imagination and skill. Suspended scaffoldings above the main sanctuary roof and around the steeple are even more spectacular.

Restoration Committee members are not certified inspectors, yet they must remember the rule above all rules in construction: no accidents should happen, especially personal injuries. In the case of scaffoldings, there is never too much support for an extra load, which may be a foundation sill, subfloor, ceiling, roof beams, and so on.

The scaffolding area must be bordered with red plastic fences so no children or animals climb on it. Yellow warning tape stating "keep off" must be everywhere around the scaffoldings. All building entrances and exits must be protected with solid roofs from above scaffoldings.

If the scaffolding is inside the church, special questions arise for the committee members: what to do with it during the Sunday service—take it down, move it to one side, leave room underneath for people to pass and sit at the pews? Or is it better to close the church and have the service in the social hall or chapel? Indeed, scaffolding is a main concern for everyone involved in the restoration project.

If other contractors must use the same scaffolding to do their jobs, they must sign waivers and assume all risks for using someone else's scaffoldings.

FOUNDATION

It is this area where you are most likely to find something wrong during any inspection. Many churches have a rudimentary foundation with large stones arranged on top of one another and splashed with mortar between their cracks. To judge the extent of foundation damages and to determine how to correct them is a delicate task and often just a "shot in the dark." You may need to replace the entire foundation or parts of it, or you may end up spending a lot less money by fixing and not replacing it. It all depends on the extent to which the Restoration Committee needs and wants to repair the foundation.

Before even doing the inspection, it is important for the committee members to do the best possible research on the church's history.

Some basic questions must be answered: When was the original foundation built? With what materials? Were there any later improvements or additions, any parts replaced? Was any other foundation built on top of the original one? Where are drainage plans or any other original plans?

Try to find the reasons for cracks, fissures, gaps, and missing parts in the foundation, especially near the corners. Just as in any walls, some of the cracks may indicate a building settlement, poor bonding between the supporting layers, an overload, or similar problems. As a rule, any crack leads to a problem; the longer the crack, the more attention must be paid.

Answering any of these problems will help define the state of the current foundation. If any of these questions cannot be answered, it is a good idea to have a vertical strip of foundation dug up way below the bottom of it. The best part to excavate is the one that sinks, crumbles, or leaks the most.

After washing the exterior wall, the exposed foundation tells an interesting story. The way the wall was built tells how deep the foundation really is, the number of stages in which it was built, the kind of materials (especially the nature of the mortar), and how strong the foundation currently is.

Once I was involved in restoring a church foundation whose corner kept sinking into the ground. After digging deep along the foundation, we discovered the reason. The foundation that could be seen from inside the basement, which we believed to be the real one, was in fact built on top of a much earlier foundation. That first foundation was built with large round stones, but without mortar. Because of the weight of the church and its settlement, some of the stones moved and the original foundation began falling apart, pulling down the newer foundation. This happened more than a hundred years after the two foundations were combined.

In another case, the foundation mortar simply began to turn into powder, and the stones lost their grip with each other. The foundation seal sagged, the walls began to crack, and the tower lost its verticality. In both cases the foundations had to be replaced.

As a rule, if more than 40 percent of a foundation needs to be re-placed, the entire foundation should be replaced. It is best to dig new and larger footing and pour an iron-reinforced foundation under the church.

A foundation scope of work will organize all the activities involved in building a new foundation for a church sitting on large boulders:

1. Clean up the crawl space under the church to make room for work.

2. Install temporary cement block legs next to the main supporting rocks to secure the steadiness of the church structure.

3. Dig around the same supporting rocks to reach the firm soil underneath.

4. Jack up the church to make room for the new sill and support-ing pillars.

5. Make plywood forms and assemble the steel structure for each leg/pillar, as specified in blueprints. Do the same with the sup-porting rocks/boulders.

6. Pour concrete into the leg forms and around folders to reach the new upper line of the foundation. Let the cement dry. Pour concrete foundation between legs. (See pictures 13 and 14.)

7. Install the new sill on top of the new foundation. Flash it properly.

8. Build a new access door to the crawl space for eventual storage or a utility room.

9. Replace all rotten beams or trim and reinforce them with two-by-eight-inch or thicker beams. All new joists, new wood, and subfloor will be treated with wood-preservative solution.

10. Carefully lower the church frame onto the new foundation, which will make the building sound and free of any further movement.

Obviously, to replace a foundation or even a sill is a major and dif-ficult job. It begins with lifting the church. The Restoration Committee is responsible for asking the contractor about the plans

Picture 13 (top) and 14 (above). *This is a typical example of a foundation with a rotten sill, from under which stones slipped away and cement blocks were placed to hold the building corner. This restoration starts with digging a new foundation and building an enforced concrete pillar and a new sill of solid beams. Later on, the space between the new pillars will be filled with cement or a stone foundation.*

for lifting and replacing parts of the entire foundation. If several solutions are presented, the committee must decide which to go with—which is least damaging to the building and most reasonable for the budget.

"Shoring" up a foundation means taking the weight of the building off the foundation and providing a temporary support for it. The next operation is the "needling," which requires extra beams to add strength to the lift. Any jacks used must be placed on firm ground, resting on large wood blocks that will spread the weight evenly. It is the same principle as lifting a car except that a foundation should not be lifted more than a quarter of an inch from above the original line.

The committee members must also watch the jacking of their church and stop the process any time they feel that something might go wrong. There could be uneven lifting, noise from the disjointed building, walls cracking, windows breaking, and many other clear signs of damaging the church.

The removal of the old foundation and any type of "underpinning" (replacing of portions of the foundation) must be done in small and alternating sections. A highly qualified building engineer or a specialized architect must determine the size of these sections. Because of the obvious danger involved, while workers remove parts of the old foundation, a committee member must watch their work. Workers can be the best, but their effort and concentration is directed to their work, not to what happens to the rest of the building. Jacks and other materials must be ready to stabilize the building in the event of an unexpected structural move.

The best procedure is to work under one wall at a time, instead of digging and replacing the entire foundation.

If only the sill has to be replaced, the committee members must remember that it supports the entire building structure. A sill may look good if inspected only from inside the basement, but once the outside trim is removed, the same sill may show serious damage. When a healthy sill is hit with a sledge hammer, it will produce a high-pitched sound. A rotten sill will have a muffled sound.

To replace a sill or parts of it is a hard and time-consuming job. All decision makers must choose how and where to set up the hydraulic jacks. They can be (some thirty to forty feet apart) under the sill, above it, or pushing up the wall at an angle to free the sill.

Any jack plates must lift a strong stable point that holds the structure in place. A lift must correct all the sagging lines that occurred when the old sill collapsed, even if they are hardly noticeable.

White oak is probably the best choice for a new sill (eight-inch to ten-inch square timber). Many contractors opt for pressure-treated beams. Any holes should be drilled slowly and screws should be waxed or soaped to ensure smooth penetration when securing the overlapping sill beams.

In any case, the new sill must match the size of the old one and the lift must be just high enough to slip the new sill in its place. This is the best time also to fix and reinforce the timber, including the subflooring, from above the new sill.

Before covering the sill with trim or siding, a professional extermination contractor must be called to preventively treat with insecticides the entire exposed timbers.

To prevent structural or cosmetic damages, the wall on the new sill should be lowered in the same gentle manner as when jacking it up.

Interior Moisture

This is a stubborn enemy of any foundation or basement, and water problems seem to be the most common source. Brick, stone, and concrete are water-absorbents. Often the mortar finish is done only in the interior of a foundation, or not at all, leaving the foundation unprotected.

Moisture is easy to smell, feel, and see, in the form of a damp odor, marks on stone or brick walls, dark stains on wood, moist spots on floors, and in the dampness of the stored objects. Wooden doors and windows swell and cannot be closed any longer. They can be washed and bleached to reduce their damp smell, but this does not eradicate the moisture. The presence of water in a basement may be unavoidable.

The ideal cost-effective antimoisture job is to find the leaking spot and seal it. But sometimes that spot is close to impossible to find because water, just like wind, seems to penetrate in mysterious ways. There are some preventive steps to take to stop a leak into the basement, however, and they should be tried before undertaking major foundation jobs. The first step is to eliminate any roof water saturating the foundation and any swampy ground from the sprinkler system or other sources.

This is easier said than done because water's capillarity is nature's law. Water rises on walls and carries with it fertilizers and salt (from melting snow) that attack the mortar and weaken the foundation. Special waterproofing chemicals are often injected into foundation walls to prevent moisture from spreading inwards, or caulking sealants are used to fill any gap inviting water inside. Expanding foam fillers are sprayed around the pipes and window or door frames, and even mortar is used on top of that to stop water.

Because water cannot be controlled too much, from the very beginning people chose a dry or a high piece of land on which to build. They still do, to discourage water intrusion into their dwellings. Over

time they have come up with additional defense systems, such as digging open trenches to collect the water from uphill, or building
drainage around a structure. But over the years, acid rain, which reacts with lime mortar, has eroded foundations. On top of that, frozen
water trapped in cracks opens channels for vegetation roots that cause
leaks. Water falling from the roof straight into the foundation ground
completes the picture of moisture damage.

Prewar technology introduced black tar paper and pink "builder's
paper" as moisture barriers. But these created wood rot and encouraged insect nests underneath. Later, "housewrap" materials allowed
moisture to pass while keeping away cold and heat. Today, versions of
vapor barrier/retarder made out of plastic or foil-based products are
available to double the foundation insulation.

If the foundation has an in-ground water problem, the church
committee members must take time and identify the source of the
moisture. Questions to be answered are:

- Is it permanent or temporary seepage? Does it happen only
  when it rains or when snow melts?

- Is the moisture or water coming from outside or inside the
  basement?

- Is there a drainage system in place that fails to function?
  Is it clogged so that the water simply cannot exit?

- If so, can the clog be fixed? Where is the problem?

- Is outside water backing up into the existing drainage?

- Is the entire foundation sunk in water?

- If you need to excavate around the foundation, then how much
  and how deeply?

- Should you build an entirely new drainage system or just replace
  part of it?

- Does drainage exit freely, or should a dry well be dug to collect
  the water?

Answering these questions will help the contractor recommend
the best solution to the problem. He or she will also be more likely

not to be lured by a fast-talking sales representative trying to sell "guaranteed products" to prevent moisture or stop a leak. In reality there are only limited quick solutions to fix water problems.

It is ideal to find the exact root of these problems and correct them properly. But just like water problems, a leakage spot can be very deceptive when it comes to locating its source, for water travels in mysterious ways. One thing is sure: water and moisture around the foundation must be stopped before reaching the basement wall!

On the other hand, interior-produced moisture causes are multiple, ranging from vapor condensation to plumbing leaks and the lack of ventilation.

However it is produced, moisture remains the main reason for peeling paint, falling plaster, deteriorating masonry, and wood rot. It also creates fungus and mold and attracts insects.

"Demolition insects" include termites, carpenter ants, and woodboring beetles. Some thirteen different kinds of termites are known, and their shelter tubes can be found even in brick walls. Often the infested wood looks normal until it collapses.

The church must periodically hire a termite exterminator who will use various methods to destroy any insect infestation. The chemicals used are highly toxic, and all recommended precautions must be followed to the letter while restoration workers are on the site.

Ventilation and humidifiers do a great deal to correct interior moisture. But a "parging" of two coats or layers of cement or mortar on the interior walls will seal the wetness. A coat of waterproof oil paint on top of that will plug the pores. It may not work to perfection, but it certainly reduces wetness. Yet, to waterproof the foundation from the interior is like sealing a leaking boat only from the inside.

The real solution for eliminating moisture in the basement is to waterproof it. Start by digging around the foundation to uncover it entirely. Thoroughly wash the foundation and brush the dirt from it. Let it dry.

Just like building a new foundation, fixing an old one requires looking underneath it to see what kind of drainage system is in place. Most likely, the moisture in the basement comes from drainage failure, and the foundation is sunk in water.

The inspection may reveal clogged or crushed drainage pipes or pipe joints disconnected or faultily connected from the very beginning by negligent workers. Roof drainage connected to the foundation drainage can be another problem. A water vein could find its way under the foundation and practically flood the foundation nonstop.

As a rule, water sitting under the basement floor will rapidly crack it, and water will filter through these cracks. This is probably the worst damage to a foundation. An amply sized drainage system under and around the basement must be built immediately. It should consist of the roof and foundation drainage pipes, one on top of the other, well-pitched away from the church and nested in crushed stones.

Use perforated polyvinyl chloride (PVC) pipes laid with the holes facing down into the gravel to collect the water. The drainage pipes must be at least two feet under the basement floor level. The roof drainage pipes must be two feet under ground level, so they can be easily inspected, repaired, and replaced.

Once the foundation has been dug out and washed, all the decayed mortar must be replaced around the stones, bricks, or cement blocks in an old-fashioned way: by using a hammer, chisel, and trowel. Mortar is often a mixture of one part cement, three parts lime, and ten parts sand. But masons have their own recipes, as they judge the real needs of the "tuck-pointing" job while replacing decayed mortar.

A mason will use the same judgment while parging the foundation from outside, in a similar fashion to that described for inside. The outside parging cement layers can be thicker, going one-half inch in the bottom and ending one-quarter inch from the top, which must be at least one foot above ground level.

Many masons go one step further to waterproof the foundation, applying layers of hot tar and parging.

Whatever is done to waterproof the foundation, the aesthetics should be kept in mind; in other words, the improved foundation should look like it belongs to the rest of the church.

DEBRIS REMOVAL

The dumpster is a very useful thing to have while demolishing walls, removing roofs, or disposing of any large debris. Often churches instruct the contractor on how to secure the dumpster, as in this example:

> All debris shall be collected and placed into a dumpster located no closer than fifteen feet from any building or combustible structure. Dumpster will not be allowed in the garden area. The owner's representative and the contractor will determine the location of the dumpster. All debris shall be removed from the site as soon as practical. Dust generation shall be kept to a minimum. The cost of the dumpster and the removal of the debris from the site is included in the contract. Disposition shall be in accordance with local, state, and federal regulations.

A few rules for how to use the container must be observed by any contractor and enforced by the church Restoration Committee:

- The grass or pavement must be protected by providing strong board for the dumpster to be lowered to the ground, and also when the dumpster is hauled away.

- The dumpster shall never represent a hazard in any way.

- The dumpster should not be overloaded. Do not pile junk above the upper line of the dumpster; otherwise the driver may ask the contractor to have the dumpster partially emptied, may refuse to haul it, or may even empty the entire contents and leave with the empty dumpster.

- The dumpster should be filled only with what it was hired for. Iron should never be mixed with plaster, bricks, roofing material, and wood unless the dumpster's owner knows about it. Specific debris goes to specific landfills. Load the containers neatly.

- Flammable materials should never be thrown into a dumpster, not even cigarette butts.

- The area around the dumpster should always be kept clean.

- Access to the container should not be blocked. Keep a clear path for its removal.

8

Restoration can be a confusing process, with very many elements at play at the same time. This chapter will give you explicit descriptions of what to look for. Each entry should be reviewed and considered for your particular restoration needs. This will help you write the many points of the scope of work.

INTERIOR RESTORATION

Plaster

An old-fashioned cover for walls and ceilings, plaster is made of quick lime mortar mixed with sand, water, and hair or straw. Most antique and vintage interior churches are built with such a plaster, which for thousands of years was a reliable and aesthetic construction material.

Cracks in a plaster wall are normal since the wall may have been a supporting wall for hundreds of years. Some cracks are decorative, some are structural. Most decorative plaster can be cleaned and repaired using joint compound. But structural plaster, including loose plaster, must be opened and repatched with real plaster.

If the entire piece of plaster must be removed and rebuilt, follow the checklist below for the scope of work:

Sanctuary Main Ceiling

1. Supply and erect wall-to-wall scaffolding.

2. Build a plywood wall-to-wall floor at a convenient height for men to work and to permit the collection and disposal of debris. The floor must be high enough to prevent damage to pews below.

3. Supply and install plastic curtains to protect the church organ, piano, and organ pipes from dust infiltration. The owner's representative will advise on an acceptable method of accomplishing the above, and he or she will be present during this phase of the work. Pews and floors should be sealed to protect them from dust. All doors should be sealed to prevent migration of dust to other areas of the building.

4. Cut ceiling around the perimeter, one inch away from the existing cornice molding.

5. Take down plaster ceiling. The wood lath will remain. Debris should be chuted to a dumpster located in the roadway alongside the sanctuary.

6. Check the ceiling wood, framework structure, beams, and lath. Renail and replace any loose or broken lath. Any major replacement of wood beams, other than lath, will be at owner's approval and expense.

7. Install galvanized wire mesh. The mesh shall be fastened with one-inch galvanized screws into the lath, and two-inch screws into the beams. Spacing of the screws is to be between six and seven inches. Galvanized washers are to be used with the screws.

8. Apply a first light coat of plaster consisting of one part sand and one part cement. This is followed by a brown coat consisting of nine parts sand, two parts lime, and one part portland cement. The second coat will be approximately one-eighth to one-quarter-inch thick, and this should bring the ceiling close to matching the elevation of the original ceiling. The third coat will be a brown coat of portland cement of the same formula as the second coat. The purpose of the third coat is to level the ceiling.

9. Fill in and tape between the newly plastered ceiling and the old one-inch ceiling left attached to the cornice molding.

10. A final coat will be a mixture of plaster of Paris and joint compound. At this point, the ceiling shall match the level of the previous ceiling around the perimeter, and it should be properly leveled and smooth.

11. The paint should not be applied to the finished ceiling until it is fully dry, and not sooner than 30 days after plastering is completed. Plastered surfaces should be lightly sanded before applying primer.

12. Apply one coat of water-based interior primer and two coats of acrylic latex interior paint. The primer should be latex enamel undercoat, Benjamin Moore #34500. The finish coats shall be Benjamin Moore flat latex #215. Color will be specified shortly. All paint is to be brush-applied, and light sanding should be done between coats.

Ceiling under the Balcony

1. Supply and erect scaffolding over the pews along both walls, running the length of the sanctuary. Scaffolding should not touch the pews at any point. A plywood floor is to be built along the length of the sanctuary, equal in width to the balcony ceiling at both sides. Build a similar scaffolding under the balcony along the width of the sanctuary at the entrance to the sanctuary.

2. Erect plastic curtains from ceiling to floor along the interior edges of the balcony to minimize dust settling outside the scaffolding areas.

3. See "Plaster," "Sanctuary Main Ceiling," step 5.

4.–6. Continue, following steps 6–8 under "Plaster," "Sanctuary Main Ceiling."

7.–8. Refer to steps 11–12 under "Plaster," "Sanctuary Main Ceiling."

Sanctuary Walls

Follow the same procedures as for "Sanctuary," "Ceiling under the Balcony."

The preceding scopes of work tell how a plaster job must be done. But there is more to it because each job is different and plasterers have their own methods. There are many textured plaster finishes, but all have in common the system of applying with a trowel three coats over the wood (or wire mesh) strips. Nowadays, because of the high-tech methods that are available for building rooms, an old-fashioned plaster worker is difficult to find, and that skill is unique and to be admired. The old-fashioned plaster worker is able to do everything from mixing the necessary ingredients on the spot to applying the final coat.

The first coat, also known as the "scratch coat," is a rough plaster applied to the lath with a broom in order to ensure a firm grip for the next coat. It is necessary to reinforce the wood lath with nails and apply a wire mesh to it for a better grip for the future plaster. The lath must be moistened with water before the application so that the moisture from the plaster will not be absorbed into the wood. This layer of plaster is a rough coat of less than one-quarter inch, highly unattractive but durable. When it has dried after two days, any irregularities must be leveled with a scraper.

The second coat, or "brown coat," of plaster is to be applied to small areas and "feathered" with a long slicker into an even coat of about one-eighth inch. When it dries, it will resemble the whitish color of mud, which gives it the nickname "mud coat."

The third coat is applied to larger areas, previously moist, with continuous wide strokes to ensure a smooth coat. It is a highly skilled job to be done with a trowel. After the plaster dries evenly, it will be necessary to "sand" it with a wet, rough sponge. Any irregularities are to be smoothed with sandpaper. Sanding dry plaster is a messy job and workers must wear protective goggles and a breathing mask.

The plaster must "heal" for at least one month in order to balance its composition. If it is summer, fans must be provided for ventilation. If it rains, the windows should be closed and a constant temperature of 60 degrees Fahrenheit maintained. Any deviation from these drying rules will cause cracks and damages to the plaster.

Today old plaster is frequently coated with plaster of Paris, a white powder made from gypsum combined with water, which forms a quick-setting paste for casts and molds or fine patchings. It is used to reattach or replace a plaster ceiling and walls. Plaster of Paris was once used to create the unmatchable ornamental plaster along ceilings, around chandeliers, and other wonders of workmanship in plaster.

Now "dryvit" and other imitation plasters come ready-to-use in buckets. Many churches, however, prefer to have the walls and ceiling done in real plaster.

Another quick and inexpensive substitute for real plaster is sheetrock, a drywall with a gypsum core sandwiched between heavy paper. It comes in large panels that have to be custom cut and nailed, the joints filled with compound, then taped over, skim coated, and sanded.

Drywall is more of an easy "do-it-yourself" job and cannot possibly be compared to the beauty and durability of an old-fashioned plaster wall. Plaster is smooth, rich in substance, and easy to mold to any form of shape. Sheetrock shifts easily, nails and tape pop out of it, and it looks cheap. But it can be painted the day after installing it.

A veneer plaster/blueboard and skim coat can be used with a coat of real plaster troweled over it. But an experienced plasterer is needed to do the job correctly. It must show no joints and have a rich texture, and it will be ready to be painted in a few days.

Rehanging the plaster means to reattach the sagging plaster to the original line. Usually it is done on the ceiling, where gravity pulls the plaster away from the lath. Plaster has its own flexible limits; to check it, one must push it back with a flat palm. Poking cracked plaster with a hammer handle or stick will result in the collapse of the plaster.

If the hanging area accumulated debris in the empty space behind the ceiling, you must find a way to vacuum clean the loose stuff in order to ensure a tight reattachment to the lath. A commercial vacuum cleaner must be used because the fine plaster dust will damage a regular vacuum cleaner.

Reattachment can be done in two ways: by injecting bonding adhesive or by pinning the area with washers. The first method requires drilling holes (not larger than one-quarter inch and no more than six inches apart) into the hanging plaster. This requires a gentle technique because the drilling must stop before it reaches the lath. If the drilling is done from the attic, then only the wood will be penetrated, but the plaster will remain untouched. It is a blind operation that depends exclusively on the worker's feel and experience.

After the holes are drilled, a caulking gun is used to inject vinyl floor adhesive (acrylic or latex adhesive may do the job as well) between the plaster and the lath. Flooding too much adhesive does not provide a stronger reattachment. To the contrary, it will act like an extra layer between the lath and the sagging plaster. One good squeeze of the caulking gun will do it. Immediately wipe away any extra glue that comes out of the hole before it hardens.

Once the injection is done, prop the area with wide plywood pieces spread with a layer of poly so as not to stick to the plaster. You will need to push the plaster back to the original line by using shores nailed to the floor or a scaffolding platform. Gently remove the plywood after no less than twenty-four hours, when is safe for the attached ceiling to be unsupported.

The second method is to attach the plaster back to its original line by using washers or buttons. It can be used only if the plaster is solid and no debris is behind it. Because these washers are only one inch in diameter, they have limited capacity to hold the ceiling. If screwed too tight they may crack the plaster, and yet the screws must find solid lath in which to hold. The washer heads must be set inside the plaster so a few skim coats can cover them. After sanding and painting, the fixed area must look perfect.

Indeed, some bulges in plaster are so cracked and damaged that their life is over. Preparation for patching is very important and consists of cutting the damaged plaster around firm edges, nailing wire lath over the wood lath, and mixing a good plaster composition to match the old one.

Before applying the plaster, the lath must be wet, and depending on the thickness of the original plaster, one or more coats may be needed to match the original line. Adding too much plaster at once may result in the drop of the new plaster. After painting, a good patching job is virtually undetectable from the rest of the ceiling.

Fixing and patching small areas is done with plaster of Paris the way painters do the taping between the sheetrock and corner joints.

Pressed Metal and Other Ceilings

These ceilings with their Victorian patterns were the marvels of their time, similar to how plastic ceiling tiles are for us today. Highly decorative and rust-free, the tin-plated steel squares can be stripped, primed, and painted just like a plaster ceiling.

Very often, metal ceilings were covered with sheetrock, another revolutionary invention of cheap and fast construction material. But there is no comparison between the two rival products because the metal ceiling proved to be a clear winner with restoration lovers.

Churches with metal ceilings are rare, and congregations may consider restoring it for a few good reasons: durability, beauty, and easy maintenance. After all, a metal ceiling is a novelty to be proud of.

Modern mass-produced goods have had a huge impact on the restoration business. Among the most popular products is nontoxic polyurethane paste, invented to replace the marvels of plaster work. It is easy to use for fixing floral designs, column capitals, moldings, and other architectural embellishments.

The traditional American wood-framed church has no painted walls or ceiling. Some Catholic and Episcopal churches, such as Christ and Holy Trinity Church in Westport, Connecticut, are rare exceptions, and their restoration requires an artist rather than a plasterer or a painter. Greek and Russian Orthodox churches with their wall and ceiling paintings are obvious art works that remain untouched for many generations.

Ceiling vaults, regardless of whether they are made of wood, stone, or marble, play a major supporting role, along with the mission to enhance the upper structure. In all cases, they bear the signature of the architect or the craftsperson who designed and installed them in an irreproachable style. To fix them takes a team of expert carpenters or masons, plasterers, and painters. Any replacement in continuity of a vault is a difficult job and must be treated like replacing part of the foundation.

Carpentry Work

Carpentry is very important for any building restoration, and indeed, each time one turns around, some woodwork must be fixed. Because the work is so highly specialized, a contractor may hire outside carpenters for structural work, floor and steps, doors and windows, and fine carpenters for column cornice and floral work, sanctuary furniture, and many others.

Beam repairs are a basic job of primary importance: beams secure the entire building structure and hold it together. Because our forebears did not have pressure-treated lumber, beam damage is caused by rot, insects, structural shifting, thermal moves, pressure cracks, joint failure, and other things.

The committee members must be aware that no guesswork is allowed when dealing with beams. Beams play too important a role, such as holding up a tower, roof, bearing wall, a ceiling, or a floor loaded with hundreds of people. An engineer or an architect must be hired to decide why a beam is falling and what to do to fix it. These people also know building codes and local rules and regulations related to correcting the damages.

Beams are indeed the "backbone" of the church. Just taking the roof as an example, we can see an intricate structure of the beams supporting the ridge, rafters, purlins, and other essential lumber.

The importance of beams is evident in their names: tie beam, dragon beam, king post, queen post, crown post, and others.

Common ways of reinforcing a beam are to replace the failing portion or to "sister" it. Replacement of beam segments often includes jacking of the designated area so its supporting role will be replaced. The new replacement must be of the same wood size and density (but pressurized) and enforced with heavy braces.

To "sister" a beam is to double it with a similar one, on one or both sides. There are many ways to do it, but just one firm rule: always bolt the "sisters" over a steel plate or steel angles; never just nail them together. The bolts (with washers) must be lined up in alternate order so their holes do not line up and crack the beam. Drill holes in the center of the beam to make sure they do not split the beam.

Before any assembly, treat all beam surfaces with wood preservative solution. In the past, the end of the beams were "fire-cut," to make them moisture- and insect-proof. It really worked. Today, most heavy beams are treated with preservatives.

Pay special attention to the beam pocket in a brick or stone wall, to be sure it is large enough for resetting in a solid support. Look for the beam curvature and make sure it will face upwards. In time, the load from above will push it into a straight line.

Note that a steel beam is not much stronger or longer-lasting than an oak beam. I have seen churches consumed by fire, with steel beams melted or curled in unusable ways. Next to them were ten-by-ten-inch (or thicker) wood beams that burned just on the outside but stayed in place and probably remained stronger than before. They are immune to water or insect penetration. Also, wood beams do not need to be painted and they will not rust.

Arches and Vaults

Arches and vaults must be treated with special care because they carry a lot of load and hold vital structural parts together. Semicircular, triangular, Venetian, Florentine, oblong, rib, or any other form of arches and vaults represent the best of beam workmanship. However, their exceptional lines of dazzling designs and embellishment seem to hide their equally exceptional strength and supporting role.

Just because they are so beautiful does not mean they are superficial fixtures. Overlooking that can be dangerous when restoring them. Any work done on arches and vaults must be performed from scaffoldings. Any jacking must be treated as lifting the roof or a foundation sill, only with much more care, because arches and vaults are more likely to crack and break than any other wood structure. A neglectful lift can also induce stepped cracking on the bearing walls and ceiling.

A whole book can be written about the richness and variety of the moldings, which are abundant in any church. For sure, all eighteen types of moldings with names as intricate as their design (cock bead, rope torus/twisted cord, fluted torus, reeded torus, reed and tie, quirk bead, dentil, corona, reverse ogee, etc.) always found a beautiful use inside churches.

The presence of ornamented motifs and ornaments themselves, devices, heraldic devices, and arabesque are even richer, and they are done in wood, stone, or marble.

Wood epoxy and small wood replacements described in a later chapter on wood restoration are applicable to all of the above wood ornaments.

The same repair principles are applied to the rest of the beam family: girders, headers, joists, rafters, and so on, subflooring included.

Floors

Because subflooring was used in America only after 1900, church floors are typically built from heavy planks nailed across beams. If hardwood floors were installed later, they might squeak, for they do not lie perfectly flat. To correct a squeak, wedges must be tightened under the subfloor from below, and the same operation applies to the stairs. Even though plywood is squeak-resistant, not too many churches will install it as a subfloor. Certain things just do not fit with church tradition.

The beams under the floor may need to be jacked up and supports or columns should be installed under it. As described earlier, any lifting must be done very gently and in many stages. Never overjack a floor. Any supporting posts must rest in concrete footings.

Floors come in a wide variety of materials. Newer churches may have elegant parquet floorings with plain English, Brixton, or even mosaic designs.

Unlike in a private house, church floors are made of heavy planks (of oak, chestnut, maple, redwood, and other resistant wood) nailed next to each other or engaged in tongue-and-groove edges. Their imperfections make them unique, attractive, and trustworthy.

For that sturdy reason, no fine carpentry is needed and less sophisticated restoration is required. Basically, you will need only to fix the creaks, put wood putty in small holes or cracks, and replace missing pieces.

Squeaks are silenced by hammering wedges back into place, or with screws anchoring loose boards from below or above. Long nails must be driven in a "V" direction into the joists. Just like fixing columns and windows, wood substitutes, structural adhesive paste, liquidwood, and wood epoxy can be used to restore wood floors.

Floor shrinkage is only natural, and it should not bother anyone because flooring is not structural. Hemp rope soaked in linseed oil or glue, and sawdust mixture with glue can seal gaps in the same manner that sailors fix their boats. Wider gaps may require glued wood strips, finely shaped to fit faulty lines.

If wood replacement is needed, selecting the proper wood is a difficult job. To match old woodwork, contractors often go to wreckage places to find pieces rescued from demolition of vintage houses. If you must use new wood, it must be "aged." It takes a lot of detective work to find the right way to do it.

Replacing large parts of the floor requires a wood cured of its moisture and fully stabilized before it is added to the old floor. (See pictures 15 and 16.)

In all cases, the repaired area must be sanded in the direction of the floor grains. Any professional replacement must be almost indistinguishable.

Church floors can be also made of cement, mosaic, brick, flagstone, slate, tile, terra-cotta, marble, and other materials. A colonial American style might use a combination of traditional hardwood floor and other

Picture 15 (top) and 16 (above). *Floor badly damaged, removed to show an even more damaged subfloor, to which was added a sister joist and cement blocks to keep the floor from collapsing.*

floors. Because of the way these nonwood floors were constructed, it is common to find numerous hairline cracks on their surface. Why they are there is not important. What is important is that they stayed the same over the years and created a certain character with their cracked look. Never try to open and patch these fine cracks. If a crack is getting larger and becomes a walking hazard, then a specialist must be hired to deal with it.

To restore stairs you must hire a fine carpenter who understands the intricate geometry of the handrails, treads, risers, balusters, landings, and so on. With stairs in a quarter turn, spiral, wreath, and other shapes, it is hard to describe how a job like that must be done.

Doors

Doors are very important in a restoration project. As a matter of fact, not too many parts of a church suffer more abuse from people, time, and weather than these truly functional and ornamental works of fine and durable carpentry.

Church doors were made in a limited variety: panel, swing, and double swing. These types of doors provide an entrance and exit for a large number of people. Because of that, their obvious problem is their size and weight, which bring a lot of wear and tear.

An old church door is indeed a work of art, and often its setting has most of the architectural elements included in it: curved brackets, posts, front steps, canopy, cornice, lintel, header, jamb moldings, panels, weatherboard, threshold, even windows.

Before making any decision, committee members must inspect the doors to see if they fit properly, if any of the wood is rotten, and if there is any damage or other malfunction. Tightening a screw, readjusting a hinge, and renailing some parts may solve the entire problem.

Before cutting or reframing a door, you must determine why it resists closing, drags on the threshold, has gaps everywhere, or has a lock that doesn't work. The door may not need to be taken down and pulled apart as the contractor wants to do, but some parts may need minor adjustments. Again, never rush to cut a door. It is better to make a mistake with its frame than with the door itself, which in most cases is irreplaceable. How to strip, stain, or paint a door is described in the upcoming "Exterior Restoration" section of this chapter.

But unless it is protected by a roof or a similar cover, a massive exterior door takes unusually harsh punishment from sun, wind, and rain. Many coats of stain or paint must be added to protect a door that is exposed to outside elements. Building a roof over the main doors will extend their lifespan and exquisite look.

Today, building codes impose fire and panic alarm attachments, and these sometimes even require changing the door so that it opens toward the outside. In one case, all those safety measures were included during a restoration project, and the parishioners were happy with the modern changes. During a snowstorm that piled the drifts against the entrance doors, however, the worshipers could not get out of the church. A few of them climbed out a window and shoveled the snow to open the doors for the rest. Only then could the trapped people walk out of their church, as updated as it was according to the latest code of safety.

From this story, one may wonder how little could be done to improve what the original builders knew too well without too many rules and regulations.

Other Restoration
Windows

Church windows are as glorious looking from outside as from inside. There are more than twenty window types incorporated in church architecture, and their names are self-descriptive: lancet, dagger, mouchette, trefoil, quatrefoil, multifoil, rose, geometrical, intersecting, reticulated, curvilinear, panel, and others. All of them provide light inside the church rather than serving those inside to look outside of it. Only some windows pivoting horizontal or vertical, hopper or louvered, awning or double hung, are built to close and open for ventilation. The rest are fixed into the wall, for they are too large and heavy to play with.

In most old churches, the sash/double-hung windows are over-sized, yet they can be handled with ease. The ease is facilitated by the sash-weight principle, whereby the pulleys work both ways: to hold the window open and to reduce the handling effort.

That weight attached to the ropes is proportionately heavy to the size of the window. If this system is stuck or broken, the braided cotton cords must be replaced with nylon ones. They do not get wet and they are more resistant to friction. To detach, attach, and balance the weights and the pulleys is a specialized job, and the contractor must be encouraged to hire a professional to do it.

Indeed, to take apart a double-hung window of considerable size and weight, probably decorated with precious stained-glass panes, is a big responsibility. The general contractor, however, is very much needed to help with scaffoldings, cutting the plaster around the windows to protect the glass, and, of course, repatching and restoring walls around the windows.

Most problems with windows have to do with broken glass, glazing bars falling apart, missing caulking, and the sill and frame not holding anymore. More likely, the above dripping edge does not protect the window, causing rot and cracks. In many cases, the window must be taken out and sometimes apart. Its whole setting must be fixed or done over in a meticulous manner, with great attention to detail. And then it must be painted or stained to match the original.

A special restoration subject is offered by stained-glass windows, the "mood creators" in any church. Indeed, by using biblical stories as design themes, and bright colors projected by outside light, these windows seem to offer a glimpse into heaven.

High Gothic churches with massive walls and lateral rooms, or simple and supple colonial churches, often display large stained-glass windows filtering a kaleidoscopic light. The multicolor effect enhances the altar and sanctuary like nothing else in the world.

Periodically, the Restoration Committee must check the condition of the cames (lead lines holding pieces together) and solder joints. The common problem with these windows is deformation of the lead lines, bulging of the stained glass, and leaks around the frames.

Always hire a reputable artisan to take care of the glass part, although the leaking is part of the regular restoration project. The larger the window, the larger the leak and the more work required.

The Restoration Committee must consider first the lintel and the flashings, or the edge drip of the window as leak sources. Heavily ornate moldings above the windows may facilitate a leak. If the outside wall is brick or stone, water may infiltrate through cracks or a missing mortar point.

Even after fixing everything around the window, the leak may still be there, "bleeding" through the plaster around the window frame. Often it comes from the roof line, so always check the attic for leaks.

The best way to protect any window from breakage as well as weather abuse is to enclose it with a plastic storm window with or without a bottom portion designed to open.

Beautifully embellished hooded and crowned doors and windows add a monumental touch to any building. Along with the ornate towers or steeples, they impose a unique architectural style for any church. Their restoration in good taste and original format is a must.

Light Fixtures

Chandeliers and light fixtures really do not belong to the restoration work done by a general contractor. They are very specialized items, and it is better to work with a craftsperson or lighting specialist for these decorative and utilitarian fixtures.

Church Furnishings

These are usually beautifully carved woodwork, such as the communion table, the altar with altar rail and crosses, triforium, canopy, the pulpit, misericord seats, all kinds of screens, pews, sanctuary knockers, steps, arches, and many other things.

When refinishing furniture, use something like the following oil stain formulas:

1. Prepare the surface by completely removing the old finish and do the final sanding with 220-grit sandpaper.

2. Apply a 50/50 blend of McCloskey Tungseal Dark Walnut #1151 and Miniwax #225 Red Mahogany.

3. Allow to dry approximately fifteen minutes and wipe with clean cloth.

4. Apply a second coat to obtain a slightly deeper color.

5. Allow to dry twenty-four hours. Apply a blend of satin varnish and eggshell varnish to obtain the degree of gloss desired. (A wash coat of shellac may be applied to prevent bleeding of stain into the varnish.)

6. After twenty-four hours, sand with the finest grit sandpaper, lightly dust and clean with a tack rag, and apply a second coat. Same procedure for the third coat.

Use the following scope of work for water stains on cherry pew rails, poplar choir loft pews, and pine stair rails in the narthex.

1. Poplar and pine require meticulous care in removing all the old finish. Cherry can be sanded.

2. Lightly sponge the surface with clear water. Allow to dry for at least one hour.

3. Sand lightly with 220 or finer grit sandpaper to remove raised grain.

4. Apply Constant Water Stain Brown Mahogany #1000 with disposable polyurethane type or other brush. Wipe dry after a few minutes. You may wish to blend this stain with Walnut #1404 to

make the color somewhat less red. Use extreme care to avoid spattering.

5. After the piece is completely dry, varnish coats may be applied as in steps 5 and 6 of the oil stain instructions.

These two scopes of work were written in 1992. Though some new products have since been introduced on the market, restoration experience teaches us that the older the working procedure, the better the results it produces. Some restoration techniques remain unchanged—as icon painters agree.

Church furniture is most likely very good quality and covered with a layer of shellac, lacquer, or varnish, which will keep on looking just great. Therefore, there is no need to strip such items. Wood that has had an old finish is likely to absorb stain unevenly. Besides, the old finish can seldom be completely removed without damaging the wood.

If the furniture looks dirty, unevenly colored, or just worn out, a finish reviver will clean and rejuvenate the original splendid finish.

Cleaning a quality wood finish is easy, and various combinations of denatured alcohol, lacquer thinner, and solvent soaps are used by contractors, who must be able to judge their real uses. Many times dishwashing liquids and less concentrated mineral spirits will do the cleaning job.

When using chemicals, always test on a sample area in a less visible spot to see how the wood reacts to it. Write down the formula used. If you like the result, proceed to treat the rest of the furniture. Apply the same solution with a paintbrush or a rag, and allow a few minutes for the solvent to penetrate the old finish. Gently rub the surface with a fine steel wool pad (minimum grade). Immediately remove the dirt with rags or paper towels. The stronger the removal solution, the more wood will be revealed. Apply it uniformly.

A note of caution: make sure there is no air draft in the room, and do not use an electric fan while applying coats of staining! Any draft or air movement will bring dust into the stain mix and ruin the job.

The church committee must supervise and approve each staining step. The same worker should work on like areas in order to maintain the same quality of refinishing.

If the furniture is covered with paint, the committee must consider several reasons for it: the wood quality is poor, it is made of patches that need to be covered, or the paint was added later on. Uncovering the wood to reveal the paint underneath may give a clue of how it must be handled. As a rule, you should repaint the furniture because stripping may cost a great deal and will produce poor results.

Interior colors are more diversified than exterior colors, and it is a good idea to offer a color sample to the parishioners before painting the walls. Usually, the ceilings are painted off-white or light blue, walls in a creamy color, and the plaster or wood moldings in a pure white.

Apply paint mainly to the church trims, doors, columns, floral panels, and wainscoting, whose unique patina is the result of numerous layers of paint and age. If the old paint must be stripped by heavy chemicals (such as Peel-Away), which are highly toxic and inflammable, workers must be protected by the appropriate gear. Cross-ventilation enforced by powerful fans must clean the air. Often workers may need to use heat guns, so a fire extinguisher must be at hand.

Steel wool and rags are required to remove the stain or paint, and the floors must be protected during such sludgy jobs.

Rare woods from cherry to mahogany to chestnut are hard to find. It takes a master contractor to replace missing antique woodwork and match its grains, color, and design. Such work is very messy, but nevertheless, the result is a work of art much appreciated by connoisseurs.

After numerous treatments, the new wood should blend with the old. Test the desired color on a scrap piece of the same wood. Keep in mind that liquid stains penetrate the wood deeper and faster than a gel stain, which leaves a rich pigmentation. You may need to mix more than one stain to get the desired result.

No ready recipes seem to work, but a few rules do apply to working with all wood finishes:

- Match the line of the old cut or design.

- Detect the original stain color and try to match it.

- Work under the same light all the time.

- Match any sanding to the grains.

- Sand and stain, sand and stain again, and add highlights until you obtain a color close to the original.

- If shellac is needed, apply multiple coats until a rich gloss is achieved.

- Because everything used is highly flammable, dirty rags must be deposited in water for washing or disposal.

The Restoration Committee members don't need to learn how to do a finish job in order to follow the contractor's work. What they must do is to make sure the contractor does not overdo the stain or add more and more coats until the wood looks "just right."

Floors are stained in a similar manner.

Refinishing old floors is done in the same old-fashioned way, and the Restoration Committee must decide if the floors will be only stained and buffed, or sanded and protected by clear polyurethane. Often the church floors are already painted, so to repaint them, probably in a similar color, is the best bet for making everyone happy.

Pews and altar furniture require different painting decisions. Usually they follow the color of the previous paint.

Modern Additions

Elevators, handicap ramps, fire and theft alarms, audio systems with speakers, and other modern additions should be tailored within the ecclesiastical spirit. But they are often nothing but an eyesore in the old-fashioned setting of a secular church. There is little stranger than seeing a priest/pastor with a microphone blasting his distorted voice inside a rather small church.

A chancel, the holiest part of the church, for serving Holy Communion, must look like it is a slice of heaven, not made from hardware store supplies. From the plastic cupolas and vinyl siding to the plastic pew cushions, any intrusions of the modern take away from the mystery and comfort of the church.

EXTERIOR RESTORATION

Masonry

Brick and Stone Work

This restoration work involves replacing loose bricks, and repointing and reconditioning the existing walls.

To evaluate how damaged the bricks are, committee members must analyze the brick lines and see if individual bricks are cracked, have disintegrated, have rounded corners, or are simply falling out of place when poked. A strong brick cannot be cracked or moved by hitting it gently with a hammer. The mortar joints must be equally strong and not pulverize when scratched with a screwdriver.

Any work done to replace the brick/stone and the mortar must be done in the old-fashioned way with a chisel and hammer for vertical lines, and a power grinder for horizontal joints. A good mason uses these tools with great efficiency when knocking the old mortar out.

When replacing the bricks, one can take out no more than six bricks in a row, otherwise the brick line above it will collapse. The empty space must be cleaned of all debris and dust using compressed air or water before replacing the old bricks.

The new bricks, mortar consistency, and color must match the original, and the contractor may need to take numerous trips to the specialized depot to find the right stuff.

Repointing is necessary when the mortar line is eroded more than one-quarter inch from the face of the wall, allowing water to enter inside the building. Rain, wind, pollution, and structural settling are the causes of the mortar damage. Temperature changes and leaking gutters accelerate the opening in the joints.

To repoint brick or stone work is a specialized job since there are at least ten ways to finish the mortar joints (flash, concave, V-shaped, extruded, beaded, raked, and other). A craftsperson is required. The job starts with the right mixture of lime, portland cement, and sand, all dry. Adding the proper dose of dye to color the mortar is where the experienced contractor comes into action, who should present a sample to the committee members for approval.

Repointing takes great skill in order to press the new mortar into the empty lines so that no air pockets are left. The mortar is flashed to the wall line and then left alone for some thirty minutes before being whitewashed with a brush to blend in with the rest of the wall. A week later, the entire wall will be washed with a solution of muriatic acid (one part to five parts of water) or another brick cleaner. A generous flush with water will leave the entire wall clean.

Many brick churches choose to have the walls chemically washed before the pointing, and then covered with a coat of sealant that will preserve the beauty of masonry. The sealant is usually a water-repellent silicone solution, sprayable or paintable.

Unfortunately, not too many improvements can be done to previously sandblasted walls. In the past, sandblasting was done to strip masonry of stucco or paint, but the process removes the strong outer layer of the bricks and the mortar from the joints.

Painting the damaged brick and then sealing it may be the only solution available. Choosing the right color depends on which other colors dress the church and on its architectural design.

A note of caution: when the masonry sealer is sprayed, the strong chemicals will affect any glass it might touch. The church committee must make sure that all windows or other glass areas are covered and sealed before the brick treatment starts. Otherwise, the tainted glass will be damaged by the spray, and it will lose its transparency. Because any church has an impressive number of windows, the contractor will be asked to replace any glass damaged during restoration/repair at no extra cost to the church. If the spray also affected the landscaping around the church and any unique trees or plants die, their replacement cost will be added to the list of damages. Of course, the church will make no further payment to the contractor until the damage is corrected. The contractor's insurance most likely will not cover this cost. Such a loss of money is enough to put anyone out of the restoration business! Besides, new windows cannot possibly duplicate the antique look of handmade glass, so much admired and treasured by restoration lovers. All that loss would be a shame just because no one thought to protect the windows with plastic or tarps while the brick was sprayed.

Arches

Made of bricks or stones, church arches use wedge-shaped blocks that support or frame an opening, resting on the side walls only.

A line of arches resting on pillars or columns is called an arcade. Arches and arcades were originated by Roman builders, who also perfected them. Evidently the church, a copy of the Roman basilica, generously incorporated these features into ecclesiastical architecture. Fixing or replacing them requires an expert mason who has done this type of work before.

Steps

A very important part of church entrances, steps often are large, flat stones (plain, granite, marble, or other material) of an impressive weight cut to fit the concept of stairs. The church steps seem to be a succession of landing strips that lead to a large platform made of one massive stone, or two or three smaller stones. Due to their weight, water erosion of their bed, and the natural setting, the steps may have a tendency to get uneven, shift their lines, sink at one corner, or simply collapse and break.

The correct way to restore their original line is to remove the steps completely and build another footing, foundation, and bed for them. In other words, you must rebuild the entire step structure and then reinstall the stones in the same order as before.

This is a heavy job in all regards and requires special tools. A stone mason specialized in steps must be in charge of it.

Stucco

The outside mortar-like version of plaster, stucco is made with masonry cement, sand, and water. Each contractor has a secret formula, based on a high-lime mortar or lime/portland cement mortar.

One recipe includes a bag of hydrated lime, a shovel of white portland cement, five to six cubic feet of sand, coarse aggregate, and hair or substitute. The best hair (one pound of hair per hundred-pound bag of hydrate lime) is from cows and horses.

If the mortar is high in portland cement, then one bag of white portland cement, one-half bag of hydrated lime, six cubic feet of sand, and the rest of the materials listed above must be mixed.

For big jobs contractors use electric mixers to prepare the stucco. The hand-mixed mortar must be mixed dry with a hoe with two holes in the blade until all the ingredients are blended together. Only then should water be added and mixed again into a perfectly blended paste. For smaller jobs, most contractors prefer to use portland ready-mixed mortar that comes in different grades. A cubic foot of sand goes well with a convenient ninety-four-pound bag of mortar (type I or II). Because hydrated lime is highly dangerous, one must wear goggles, gloves, and other protective equipment.

In most cases, the old stucco coat was applied directly on the masonry work with no lath. Brick, stone, and even wood was roughly scratched or chipped, so the stucco would stick to it. Therefore, never try to take the stucco down hoping to reveal the beauty of the walls underneath. You are more likely to uncover an ugly wall.

More than plaster, stucco is the victim of water infiltration through cracks, to which is added moisture coming out of the building with no room to exit. Stucco also sucks the water from leaking gutters and from the ground.

When you do a patching job, you must remember that old and new stucco do not bond well, so water must be sprayed on the old mortar or bricks.

WOOD SIDING

In the past fifty years, perfectly good and beautiful walls were covered with vinyl and aluminum clapboards, plastic brick imitation, asbestos shingles, or other "modern" products. Naïve or unscrupulous contractors promised a maintenance-free siding that also would insulate the building and last forever. In fact, the opposite was the case: these factory-made products were subject to fast weather deterioration, trapping the moisture behind the siding and proving very volatile in case of a fire.

Unfortunately, these "marvel" sidings did little to protect the original siding, mostly made of wood, if that was not already removed. Fortunately, they often did cover architectural details that now can be brought back to life.

As in many other situations, growing ivy is one of the most damaging factors for paint, wood, and even for brick and stucco. It is not uncommon to take the shingle or clapboard down and see a "jungle" of ivy behind the old siding, whose life was shortened by the moist vegetation from outside and inside.

The committee members must evaluate the past damages and decide how to restore the old look of their church. For wood-framed buildings, a common solution is to clapboard or shingle the walls in the old-fashioned way.

Clapboards

Because clapboards were the product of the band saw, they were used in construction after 1850. Churches from a previous era were covered with various sizes of clapboards, usually rectangular, lapped, or tongue-and-groove. They were hand-rived (hand-split and hand-planed) to follow the natural grain lines, parallel to the length of the board.

Their siding exposure was as large as nine inches, which gave the building a rare and powerful look. To match that siding material, a custom order must be addressed to specialized mills. The same history applies to shingles, which are easier to make and use.

A special siding is done in panels of dazzling, beautiful patterns made of squares, hexagons, octagons, circles, fish scales, and other shapes. Most old siding passed the test of time, as it proved to be of unsurpassed beauty and quality.

Today all clapboards are machine-made in the shape of isosceles triangles, mostly eight inches long and five inches wide. The best product is quarter-sawn/resawn boards, with grains in one direction. Some of the best products are grade number one eastern white pine, cedar, poplar, cypress, and chestnut clapboards.

One determinant of quality is whether or not the wood is knot-free. Clapboards with knots are produced in huge quantities. They are cheaper because the knots "bleed" and stain the covering paint. Contractors use "kills" primer to prevent such blemishes but without lasting results.

The technique of clapboarding a wall is well known, but committee members must insist the windows and doors be framed first, and that plank joints should end on a wall stud. The method used to hide or cut the end of the clapboard and to finish corners is also a matter of choice, and the contractor should present committee members several options for consideration and approval.

An example of a scope of work for siding and painting:

1. Erect necessary scaffoldings.

2. Remove all siding, shingles, and sheathing. Remove and store shutters.

3. Inspect the exposed structural members. Contractor will make minor repairs. Any major structural damage is to be reported to the owner's attention. Major repairs to structure are not included in the present contract.

4. Owner will have the option of hiring an exterminator to inspect for infestation and to take remedial action.

5. Exposed area to be cleaned prior to any rebuilding.

6. Fiberglass insulation with a factor of R-13 shall be placed to fill the space between the studs. A foil vapor barrier will face the interior of the building.

7. Install exterior-type plywood sheathing with hot-dipped zinc-coated nails. Thickness of plywood and siding to match existing exterior wall faceline.

8. Cover sheathing with Tyvek.

9. The windows shall be flashed with copper nine inches wide. The wood base sill will be flashed with copper sheets ten inches wide.

10. Install cedar clapboards with hot-dipped, zinc-coated galvanized nails.

11. Strip paint to bare wood on all windows and frames. Replace broken sash, window frames, and muntin. Windows shall be reputtied where necessary. Caulk all door and window frames and trim with a good quality caulking compound. Patch all holes and irregularities.

12. Apply one coat of oil primer and two coats of acrylic latex paint to all wood. Soffits to be included.
13. All debris shall be removed from the site as promptly as possible.
14. Scaffolding is not to be removed until gutter and downspout work is complete. This work is to be done by others.
15. Contractor to work from 7 A.M. to ? P.M. daily (weather permitting) six days a week. Sundays and holidays are excluded.

Nailing clapboard with a single-course, two-course, or blind nailing method is also for the committee to decide. Historical research of the church era will help shape that decision. Shingle siding follows almost the same pattern as the clapboard. Many times the two go together, making beautiful siding design.

Traditional nails rust and "bleed" through wood and paint, and they should be used only for certain jobs. Even galvanized nails have a limited rust-free life. If highly visible, they must be replaced with hot-dipped (HD) nails coated with molten zinc. Best of all are nails made of aluminum, stainless steel, or zinc.

The committee members must make sure the contractor uses the nails indicated in the contract and not cheaper substitutes. If the Restoration Committee wants specific size nails, such as slimmer than regular nails, this should be noted in the contract. Otherwise the contractor may use whatever nails are on hand, and they may damage the siding.

To see and touch rusted square or triangular nails made by hand two hundred to three hundred years ago still holding strong induces a respectful admiration for the blacksmiths of the past. The committee may ask the contractor to drill holes first (spaced some twenty inches apart), and then drive in the nails, and perhaps putty over the nail holes before priming. This may hold for a while, but in the long run, the cover will fall, revealing holes in the siding.

Stripping the damaged siding gives you the opportunity to inspect the building structure underneath it. As I have emphasized throughout this book, taking the building apart is the best time to fix the wood, clean it, and spray it with insecticide.

A century ago, walls had no insulation and the siding was nailed to the studs. Thus you should also take advantage of this opportunity to insulate the building. Indeed, one of the advantages of an exterior restoration is that insulation can be added to the building in a convenient way. A variety of rolls or insulation boards can be easily put inside the "naked" walls and then covered with plywood. The plywood itself will be covered with a Tyvek or other plastic insulation, providing a sound backing for the clapboards or shingle siding.

If you are not removing the siding, then you must drill a hole between the studs to blow in insulation. Many blowable materials are available: loose fiberglass, vermiculite, cellulose (but shredded paper retains high moisture levels, attracts wood-eating insects, and is highly combustible). Choosing the right insulation for the church is another decision for the Restoration Committee.

Shingles

To do a shingle siding is slow and meticulous work, three times more expensive in labor than clapboarding. Each shingle must be hammered in by hand, as shingles vary in thickness and resistance. Each shingle has to be perfectly placed to cover the gap between it and the shingle below. The gap is necessary to allow the shingle to expand in hot weather. Workers consider the thickness of a coin to be the right distance between shingles. A chalk line will keep the shingles lined up correctly and aesthetically.

A brief but good scope of work for replacing church shingle siding and painting it is as follows:

1. Remove the shingles on the left, right, and front sides of the church.

2. Replace them with cedar shingles and paint with a prime coat of paint and one finish coat. This includes the lower portion of the steeple.

3. Correct any damage to the timbers and sheathing under the shingles, and damaged or decayed trim. Apply plywood as sheathing where necessary.

4. All sheathing to be covered with a layer of Tyvek before reshingling.

5. New shingles shall be eighteen inches, clear cedar, five inches to the weather. No exposed nails.

6. Caulk all doors and windows before putting the new shingles in place.

7. Replace the headboards over windows and doors, using a quarter-inch pitch, and install flashings using lead-covered copper.

8. Front door and surrounding trim shall be stripped, repaired where necessary, and repainted. Any moldings removed shall be replaced, or if damaged, shall be duplicated in the same size and shape as the original. This includes the drip board along the bottom.

9. Finish coat of paint shall be Benjamin Moore high-gloss white, exterior paint.

10. Powerwash and paint remaining shingles on back of the church.

11. Refuse shall be removed when job is completed.

12. Access to the church will be available through all three doors whenever possible, and definitely on Sundays.

Clapboard and shingle repairs must be done by an experienced contractor who can either glue the split wood and reattach it to the wall, or replace parts of it. The contractor must really know wood and look for a new wood to match the grains, cut, and so on.

Liquid consolidants and paste fillers, epoxy, dutchman, or wood-splice are used to correct small areas of damage. Do not use chemicals in direct sunlight. Use gloves and goggles as protection against highly toxic and volatile products. Once they have dried, sand and prime the salvaged wood to make it look just like the rest.

Caulking the exterior is a job in itself, for it is, just like painting, part of the protection, insulation, and good looks of the building. Joints, seams, cornerboards, baseboards, window and door frames, cracks, and chimney lines must be clean of any residue before they receive an elegant and functional caulking.

Any dirt and mildew must be powerwashed (pressure under 400 psi) or scrubbed with chlorine bleach. Any moisture must be dried before caulking, priming, or painting, or it will blister.

Because caulking and priming require the same preparation, the best time to caulk is after the primer has dried.

A church member should make surprise inspections during the caulking and observe how it is being done, especially in the less visible areas of the building. This inspector must look at caulking tubes to make sure they are for outdoor caulking and specified in the contract. A good worker uses different tubes with different nozzle cuts for different size cracks. Asking a contractor to recaulk a badly done job is normal, and the contractor should admit the mistake.

Exterior Painting

This is probably the most appreciated and also the most criticized job of the entire restoration. Indeed, a painting job can make or break the reputation of the contractor, and it can bring joy or sorrow to church members.

For the Restoration Committee, some painting decisions are crucial: to strip the paint or not, to sand or to use chemical strippers, to replace damaged wood or patch it, to paint or stain over it.

Whatever the decisions, the outcome of a painting job depends mostly on the way workers prepare the siding or walls before applying the paint with a roller or a brush. A good and responsible contractor never paints from the ladder, but uses a full scaffolding to reach the top, which gives the painters a comfortable and safe working area. It makes a big difference when it comes to painting a large and tall church. Using cherry-pickers is acceptable for hard-to-reach spots on the roof, where scaffolding might cause damages.

Never allow painting in snow, rain, fog, or mist, when the relative humidity exceeds 85 percent or when the surfaces are damp or wet. Painting may be continued during inclement weather only if the areas and surfaces to be painted are enclosed and heated within temperature limits specified by the paint manufacturer's application and drying periods.

A sample scope of work for painting windows may summarize the entire painting work:

1. Strip paint from window sashes, muntins, and sills.

2. Replace any damaged wood where necessary.

3. Sand the frames around windows to solid surfaces.

4. Fill cracks and crevices with good caulking compound.

5. Clean all surfaces and be sure they are free of wax, grease, and water-soluble materials. Prime the windows with oil-based exterior primer and two coats of oil trim paint (same for all the frames).

6. All paint is to be brush-applied and a light sanding done between coats. Paint brand and colors will be specified.

The committee members must be extremely vigilant about inspecting the walls after the scraping, sanding, and patching is done, right before the application of primer, because a poorly prepared surface creates more problems than before.

Power or heat tools may be used to remove loose paint. It is very dangerous to use blowtorches or hairdryers. Instead, use rotary sanders with metal or sanding discs, heat guns, and electric heated plates.

The committee members must check with the contractor to determine the kind of cleaners to be used and to make sure these chemicals will be washed with water. Never paint over the dirt and let the wood dry.

If the paint is to be completely removed, then an orbital sander or chemical strippers are the solution. Organic and alkaline strippers can be used as chemical paint removers. Use a wire/nylon brush and a sponge with a bleach solution to eliminate mildew spots.

Try to avoid sandblasting the building unless absolutely necessary because it will shoot the wood siding or the brick full of holes, as if birds ate it.

To strip or not to strip is the eternal dilemma. An even bigger question is to see if the paint contains lead or not. If it does, a contractor with a lead abatement certificate must do the stripping, for such a contractor is qualified to contain the poisonous paint.

One must remember that almost every church school has a nursery or kindergarten in its building, and those children often run around the job site. To protect them and the environment is the utmost duty of any contractor. All OSHA rules and regulations must be strictly observed without exception. Certified workers must wear special protective equipment while blasting or stripping lead paint. The lead paint that is removed must be properly stored and dumped by a certified contractor.

If the old paint holds tight and its lead-based layers are cemented in the wood, then leave it alone. Sand the bubbles and cracked areas and prime them. Do not paint over "alligatored" paint. Somehow a touch-up paint job does not sound like a restoration project.

For a good and lasting paint job, stripping to the bare wood and starting fresh is the way to go. After all of the paint is off, the workers must sand the wood, make carpentry repairs by using galvanized nails, caulk the cracks and the joints, fill the holes (including nails) with epoxy fillers, and treat the wood with certain solutions to preserve its purity.

Because the industry changes quickly, I do not recommend any particular products, but the contractor knows better and may even have a homemade formula for treating the wood before priming.

When the time comes to prime, the wood must look spectacular, beaming with a fresh and healthy look. Before priming, choose primer to match the paint. Leaving the primer uncovered more than forty-eight hours is not a good idea. Two coats of primer are recommended, for the way primer binds to the wood is more important than final coats.

The best contractors will sand the siding after the primer and brush the dust before painting. Never paint on a wet board, even if it is only damp from dew, and never paint when the temperature is below 50 degrees Fahrenheit or above 90 degrees. Painting under those conditions will produce blisters, and the paint will peel prematurely.

If the siding is new, the contractor should buy it primed or the wood must be primed on both sides before being nailed. An alkyd or oil-based primer is recommended for its longer lasting qualities. Using latex paint over alkyd primer is a good combination.

The topcoats must be purchased from the same manufacturer because they will match better with the primer of the same brand.

Again, a church representative must make sure the contractor of the workers does not cut corners and use a cheaper paint. It will be even worse if they thin the paint to stretch its covering volume.

A good painter has a steady hand, smooth strokes, and an experienced eye to judge how many times to move back and forth over the same area. Painters may have favorite brushes made usually of animal hair, which they treasure by taking good care of them. Therefore, to see a painter using an old brush with the handle covered by countless coats of paint is a mark of competence, and the white outfit pastelled with colors completes the confident image. Such a painter never spills paint, has all the tools needed within reach, and does not rush through the job. This painter is highly efficient and always uses clean drop cloths. Any contractor knows that it is better to pay more to an experienced painter than to hire two new "cheap" ones who will mess up the job.

The church representative must make sure certain rules are strictly obeyed. If it is between late October and May in most northern regions, the contractor must begin painting after 10:00 in the morning and finish by 4:00 in the afternoon; otherwise, the paint will freeze. He or she also must make sure the painters reach underneath the clapboards between the shingles with their brushes, so the paint penetrates the hidden spots. Rolling the paint is acceptable for flat surfaces, such as for interior paint, but never for the exterior. Spraying can be done, but the quality will suffer and the job will not last as long (see pictures 17 and 18).

Fortunately, the Restoration Committee members do not struggle to choose paint colors as homeowners do. Only a few colors out of some 1,600 samples at paint stores are suitable for painting a church.

Hundreds of years ago, American churches were mainly painted red, then gray, and recently, white. Sometimes the shingle siding was painted in black. Many Episcopal churches still paint their doors red.

Grossly oversimplified or not, this brief history of paint carries an undeniable truth: "church colors" are always soothing and in balance. The best word to describe them is conservative—the colors underline, rather than fight, the architectural lines or details. The only bold color is provided by the shutters, which are usually black or green, and the dome, which may be painted in gold or green.

Picture 17 (left) and 18. Before and after restoration of columns, floral molding, cornice, ceiling, and siding.

When painting in black or dark colors, the contractor must use darker primer so the final coats will successfully cover it. As a rule, keep the color simple and inviting, without too much contrast.

☘

To paint or to stain is another crucial question for the Restoration Committee. Stains are mostly oil-based products with a stronger penetrating power in the wood. For doors and furniture, a transparent or semitransparent stain is most often used, as it best shows the beauty of the wood grain.

For outside jobs, solid opaque color stain is used, for it provides a stronger protective coat and lasts two years longer than conventional paint. It has a strong chemical smell, and it does not have the same beaming color and elegant finish as paint, but for churches that use mostly low-toned color, stain may be a better solution.

What is important for the restoration members is to make sure the contractor follows the label directions precisely.

As a general rule for outside trim work, churches like slow-drying white oil primer and oil paint. This durable paint is very resistant to weather. It also gives a shiny frame and balance to the church. The color of the siding is the traditional light gray or yellow, or an off-white color with calm tones.

Painting the doors and the windows is a more difficult job because it takes longer and requires more specialized preparation and repairs before priming. If a paint-stripping job is needed, the doors must be taken down, placed on sawhorses, and moved to a designated (safe) area, where the work may continue. No respectable contractor will work on vertical doors when stripping them.

A good "scope of work" for exterior doors is like this sample:

1. Remove all hardware, hardware accessories, machined surfaces, plates, lighting fixtures, and similar items that are not to be finish-painted, or provide surface-applied protection prior to surface preparation and painting operation. Remove if necessary for the complete painting of the items and adjacent surfaces. Following completion of painting of each space or area, workmen skilled in the trade involved will reinstall the removed items.

2. Clean surfaces to be painted before applying paint or surface treatments. Remove oil and grease prior to mechanical cleaning. Organize the cleaning and painting so that contaminants from the cleaning process will not fall onto wet, newly painted surfaces.

3. Clean wood surfaces to be painted of all dirt or other foreign substances with scrapers, mineral spirits, and/or sandpaper, as required. Sandpaper smooth those finished surfaces exposed to view and dust off. Scrape and clean small, dry, seasoned knots and apply a thin coat of white shellac or other approved sealer before application of white priming coat. After priming, fill holes and imperfections in finish surfaces with putty or plastic wood-filler. Sandpaper smooth when dried.

4. Apply paint in accordance with the manufacturer's directions. Use applicators and techniques best suited for the type of material being applied. Apply additional coats when undercoats,

stains, or other conditions show through the final coat of paint, until film is uniform in finish, color, and appearance.

5. Paint the backsides of access panels and removable or hinged covers to match the exposed surfaces. Finish exterior doors on tops, bottoms, and side edges the same as the exterior faces.

6. Sand lightly between each successive enamel or varnish coat.

7. Completely cover to provide opaque, smooth surfaces of uniform finish, color, appearance, and coverage. Cloudiness, spotting, dents, laps, brushmarks, runs, sags, ropiness, or other surface imperfections will not be acceptable.

It is difficult to find a more detailed scope of work for a painting job; this one can be applied to any other painting project, as well, though things can be more complicated when the old woodwork requires more than painting, such as stripping.

The stripping itself is not different from a painted furniture job, except that windows and some doors have glass panes. Some contractors take the pieces to the local strip shop for a "deep" stripping. Not only may they save money, but the job will be done right. To reglaze and fix the windows before painting is another skilled task that needs meticulous care.

The Restoration Committee members must make sure that the outside door panels will not be nailed, caulked, or sealed in any way, since they shrink and expand with weather changes. Never flood these loose lines with paint. Any caulking of the wood splits must be done with a flexible caulk. All the cracks and dents must be filled with an epoxy made of polyester fillers (see pictures 19 and 20).

Before priming, sanding is needed to create a good bond with the wood or old paint. Paint the large panels or frames first, then the middle, then the sides and edges. Brush the paint in the direction of the grain, mostly up and down. The outside color extends to the narrow hinge of the thickness of the door. Beyond that, the line must be painted with interior finish color. If the door is left in place, paint it first thing in the morning so it will be dry by the evening when it must be closed.

Picture 19 (left). *A stripped paneled door reveals the extent of damage to the door.*
Picture 20. *The same door restored by a chemical wash and epoxy fillings. Notice the brick wash and sealing job that rejuvenated the look of the walls, as well as the arched window and dentil work above the door.*

Good painters never paint under direct sunlight or in wind, and they always check painted doors and windows before shutting them. The last operation is to oil the hinges and locks. A contractor who leaves squeaky doors and windows behind is a contractor who cares very little about details and the quality of the job.

Leave doors and windows open until they are bone dry. Otherwise they will stick to the frame, which is one of the most common complaints of church members.

✿

Part of the painting job involves the iron work, usually neglected because it is assumed that iron and its paint lasts forever. Unlike bronze, brass, and copper, which change rust into a protective patina, iron oxidizes and the rust never quits attacking it.

Fortunately, modern technology provides rust converters that use the rust to create a metal primer, ready to receive a paint topcoat.

However, the rusted surface must be carefully brushed, vacuumed, rinsed with indicated chemicals, and degreased with mineral spirits. Just as for regular paint, the painting temperature must be between 50 and 90 degrees Fahrenheit.

Much of the old iron work is "hard-to-find" because not too many hand-hammering craftspersons are around to duplicate the original work. Cast iron work includes door knobs, hinges, backplates, rail decorations, medallions, roof crestings, weather vanes, lampposts, iron fence posts, gates, benches, and so on.

Window Washing

Since the scaffoldings conveniently reach all church windows, this contractor is often asked to wash the windows. And, yes, there is an old-fashioned scope of work for this job, too:

1. Remove storm windows.

2. Wash storm windows with mixture of one-third ammonia and two-thirds water, and scrub with a fine steel wood. Dry with cloth or paper towel. Repeat for inside windows. All windows will be washed twice and cleaned to the highest degree.

3. Apply glasswax or other commercial cleaner to all windows. Dry with cloth or paper towels.

4. All storm windows will be reinstalled by contractor.

If the ever-changing industry provides better recipes, try them first on a less-visible window.

This extra job is paid at an hourly rate, per window cost, or a mutually agreed-upon flat rate.

Chimneys

Standing up like massive flags above church roofs, chimneys make the bottom of the restoration list because usually chimneys last a very long time without any problems.

For the people who wonder why churches have so many chimneys, one must remind them that once all buildings were heated with stoves burning wood and coal. "Central heat" was used in antique and

vintage houses, which had chimneys built in the middle of the buildings so no heat would be wasted through outside walls. A central
chimney was also useful because it supported the entire building
around it.

Because churches were the closest American buildings to castles
or palaces, their chimneys copied castle chimney's size and architecture. In no time, chimney construction technique was borrowed by
estates and private houses. But unlike other buildings, the church did
not have a fireplace in the sanctuary. The heat came from cast-iron
stoves placed where the chimney flues were built or from a larger
stove in the basement, whose hot air was allowed through floor openings into the sanctuary. That is why it is hard to find a church chimney
stack with a collection of flues.

Today most church chimneys are boiler exhausts or simply ornamental. They need much professional care to be kept functioning and
to stand within safety limits. Periodic cleaning of the highly flammable creosote is a must.

A defective chimney is a source of major problems, so chimneys
have to be inspected from the bottom to the very top. Settling of the
building or of the chimney foundation can force the chimney to move
away from its original vertical line.

If the chimney is adjacent to one side of the building, it may move
away without too much damage. But if the leaning chimney is in the
middle of the building, it will move the roof and force the structure
to move with it.

External problems are easy to detect: cracks, crumbling bricks,
and powdered mortar force the chimney to tilt to one side, or simply
to fall apart. When a chimney collapses, it will go through the roof,
ceiling, and even the floor, smashing everything in its path.

One can guess from the chimney's appearance how past church
committees have tried to solve or delay dealing with a chimney problem over the years: the chimney might be anchored with long bars to
the roof structure in an attempt to hold it straight, or it might be
strapped all around to prevent it from falling apart. Such solutions are
only temporary, and a much bigger job is inevitable.

The Restoration Committee must determine how to correct these problems efficiently and cost-effectively. To take the chimney down to the ground and build it again is, in most cases, not necessary. A vintage chimney will have a solid construction. If the situation forces partial demolition of the chimney, then take it down to the roof line and patch the roof over it. Or go even lower, to the attic floor line, if the chimney is tilting and pulls the roof along with it.

In most cases, a chimney leak needs only a good repointing and a reflashing or a caulking job. The repointing must be done by a mason, probably using type N portland cement dyed to match the original line.

The most common problem is the crumbling mortar falling from the lines and cracked bricks splitting gaps into the chimney. A brick replacement and a repointing job not different from what was described previously must be carefully performed.

If new flashings are required, then old mortar lines must be taken out with a chisel to make room for the edges of the flashing. Brush and wet the joints and then fill them with new mortar. The flashing strip must be inserted in the center of the line and mortar pressed firmly with the finger against the flashing.

To prevent cracks, spray the new mortar line with water after a few hours, and again the next day. The other side of the flashing goes under the roof shingles, which will act as a bottom sealer.

Step flashing (sometimes covered with overlapping cap flashing) is very effective in keeping water away and decorative if repointed properly. One has to decide if aluminum, copper, or galvanized tin flashing "shingles" (usually of five-inch exposure) will be used around the chimney.

Often water penetrates between the flue and the chimney wall, causing puzzling leaks on the interior ceilings. The mason must detect that fault and apply a new mortar cap around the top of the flue with a pitched slope reaching the edges of the chimney. One common formula for mixing the needed mortar is one part portland cement and three parts fine sand.

If the chimney is not in use, its opening must be capped off to prevent rain intrusion. "Bird cages" must be affixed on top of the chimney to prevent small animals and birds from entering the chimney.

Refractory and high temperature mortar must be used to hold the inside lines. In case of a partial demolition, the chimney can be rebuilt following the original lines, with brick similar in texture and color for the exterior. For obvious reasons, a detailed picture must be taken before demolition.

Because of today's building codes, all functioning chimneys must be lined according to fire department regulations. If the chimney is used only for gas and oil-burning heaters, then the single-skin corrugated stainless steel flues can be installed inside the chimney. Different types of flues (with more resistant fireproof materials) are used for solid fuel and woodburning appliances. Note: It is true that the clay-tile liners and cement or metal liners may last for a long time. But a close inspection by a specialized contractor may reveal mortar joints and cracks and a build-up of chunks of soot as an obstruction and a dangerous fire hazard.

Here is an example of a scope of work for restoring a rectory chimney. The work is to put the two chimneys and four fireplaces in the rectory in safe and efficient working order, and to perform related work, as follows:

1. Take out the chimneys from the attic floor up. Cover the roof holes to keep out the weather. Remove and discard all debris.

2. Inspect the remaining bodies of the chimneys, in conjunction with inspection to be performed by the architect-engineer hired by the owner.

3. At the conclusion of the inspection, the contractor will inform the owner of the conditions revealed by the inspection, and recommend what needs to be done to ensure the structural integrity and the safe and efficient use of the chimneys. This recommendation will include advice on whether some other remedy should be applied. After considering the circumstances, the owner and the contractor will agree on what work the contractor will do to the section of the chimney between the attic level and the basement.

4. Build basement reinforcement for each chimney.

5. Point and seal the fabric of the chimneys, fireplaces, and chimney bases. Renovate and restore the fireplaces to first-class appearance, taking the backs apart if necessary.

6. Brace the roof by adding two two-by-four tie beams to every other existing rafter, approximately one-third of the way up the rafter.

7. Build the chimneys vertically from the attic floor. Erect scaffolding, open roof, finish and point chimneys, install rain protectors over the chimney openings, repair old roof hole, install copper flashings and any necessary roofing, and clean up and remove debris.

8. Remove the external flue, close the opening in the side of the house, and restore the external appearance.

9. Reconnect the furnace flue into one of the chimneys, so that the output of the furnace is vented up the chimney, without interfering with the safe and efficient use of either fireplace common to that chimney.

10. Clean up and remove all equipment, unused material, and debris.

The scope of work was simply written, but the work was hardly as simple. What seemed to be a rather small and limited job turned out to be a project much harder to complete and twice as expensive as originally anticipated. Regardless of how good inspectors and estimators are, it is difficult to find a scope of work with more loopholes than in chimney restoration. In the above case, the contractor ended up practically taking the entire chimneys apart and rebuilding them according to updated specifications imposed by the fire department.

At least a month must pass before the rebuilt chimney is "cured," and only then can it be used again.

The preceding description of work is not for a general contractor to do, but for a highly experienced chimney contractor. If the chimney is three feet lower than the roof line, the chimney expert must build the chimney to code. If the roof is done at the same time, a "cricket" (an elevated structural peak of waterproof material—metal, shingle, wood—

that channels water away from the chimney) must be built between the chimney and the uphill roof to protect the chimney from rain.

MOVING A CHURCH

Physically moving an older church structure, though rarely done, requires special heavy equipment.

To move anything that is built is a major task. But moving a church is a lifetime event requiring great skill from the movers and providing an astonishing thrill for spectators. Without a doubt, it is a highly specialized job and only experienced contractors should be hired to move a church.

The reasons for moving a church are motivated by the needs of the parishioners, who may wish to reposition the building on a better plot of land or foundation, and often by the will of an ambitious priest/pastor or a church patron. Many churches were lifted to allow a new and higher foundation to be built, so a larger inner space could be divided into functional rooms.

PROPERTY/RESTORATION COMMITTEE REPORT

After each major project, the Restoratioon Committee should write a report to acknowledge the job completion and also to inform the parishioners of other projects planned to improve the church property. Usually the report looks like a letter, such as the one reproduced here:

> The restoration and repair project started in 1987 was completed in 1989. The narthex was completely rebuilt, decorated, and dedicated this summer to our former rector. The replacement of the social hall was completed during the first quarter.
>
> The walls and ceilings of the sanctuary were repaired and painted by a professional restoration painter. The appearance of the church interior now is more consistent to colors that enhance the beauty of this building.
>
> A variety of minor projects were completed, including repairs on the parish house, to prepare it for occupancy by our interim pastor and his family.

The parking lot and the driveways adjacent to the church were paved last month. Previous conditions posing serious risks to both pedestrian and vehicular traffic necessitated this major expenditure.

Currently, a contract has been awarded to repair and restore the stone wall on Church Road. Additionally, a construction contract to satisfy fire and life safety code requirements has been approved, and work will commence next year on the main church building. These violations must be corrected to satisfy current state building codes.

The Property Committee is now studying and preparing construction documents for restoration work on the tower, clock room roof, cast iron bell, drainage, and remedial construction project of the church offices.

The committee extends its special thanks to Mr. John Glynn, architect, who has and continues to provide professional guidance, construction documents, and technical assistance. While there are many items still on our agenda, your committee is systematically reviewing them on a prioritized basis, and recognizes the necessity of selecting only those projects of the highest priority which must be done to conserve the buildings and the grounds.

Respectfuly submitted,
William Smith, Chairman

It seems only natural that such a report be written to explain what the committee achieved and to justify how the church money was spent in a productive way.

9

KEEPING THE CONGREGATION INFORMED

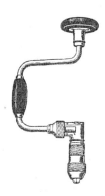

Any restoration project is an important event in the life of a congregation. It is intended to improve and beautify the building, and it is possible because of the generous donations from church members. Because of the long duration of a restoration project (on average it takes one year), it is the main discussion topic for the congregation, and everyone wants to know what is happening and how things are going. Rumors and speculations come with more or less accuracy, and the activity of the Restoration Committee can be regarded with some suspicion by people who are not properly informed about it.

The proper way to handle this situation must be addressed before, during, and after a restoration project. Even though certain details are not meant to be revealed to the general public, most of the restoration activity must be brought into open scrutiny in order to keep parishioners calm and happy.

Before the project starts and the fund-raising is launched, the committee must demonstrate the need for restoration. Because "seeing is believing," it can be most helpful to post pictures in the social hall showing the damages and even describing the importance of correcting them. Many times pieces of rotten wood or rusted metallic parts are displayed with the pictures, and sometimes large fixtures in desperate need of repairs are exhibited in front of the church.

The Sunday service bulletin and church newsletter should be used to underline and remind parishioners of the problems. Press releases may lead to an article in the local newspaper.

The pastor or the priest is certainly the right person to convey any restoration message from the pulpit to the church goers. His or her passionate plea should include some material facts in order to be convincing and mobilizing.

The vestry or other admistrative board should announce the names of the members of the Restoration Committee and leave room for comments and objections regarding their credibility and qualifications. A secret vote may not be necessary, but an open meeting to discuss the restoration project is always a good idea.

Once the restoration work begins, the curiosity of the parishioners increases. There is nothing wrong with this, but the committee needs to be aware of it and respond from time to time about the progress being made. Parishioners might be invited on a tour of the construction site but not be allowed to climb scaffoldings or expose themselves to unnecessary danger. It never hurts to have a spread of donuts and beverages to help make the inevitable problems easier to digest.

Meanwhile, the Restoration Committee should be very keen on checking the work of the contractor according to a very rigorous "punch list."

The punch list can be periodic or final. It is a must on the agenda of the church committee since, more often than not, a major restoration cannot ever be a perfect job. Some suggestions for this list include:

- Extra repairs
- Additional reinforcements
- Additional installations

- Missed spots
- Touch ups
- Changing a finish coat
- Cleaning
- Washing

A genuine punch list after a two-year restoration looked like this:

1. Exterior work

- Fix louver in the bell tower and put back window screens.
- Fix cracked windows in tower.
- Repoint tower copper flashings.
- Fix and reflash cricket beyond main chimney.
- Fix and reflash gas vent.
- Replace cracked sanctuary window and reglaze/paint it.
- Fix old roof leaders and move them in the back; install the new leaders in the front of the church.
- Fix and paint the bottom molding of the back door.
- Rebuild part of the base of the left column and paint it.

2. Interior work

- Install additional walkway in attic.
- Construct steps over air conditioning (AC) duct in attic.
- Repair knee brace in attic.
- Touch up ceiling around the new smoke detectors.
- Sand and paint AC drops in the balcony.
- Reset front pews for handicapped.
- Reinforce front pew rail.
- Secure choir seats to floor.
- Finish staining minister's and choir benches.
- Affix numbers on pews.
- Install hymnal directories.
- Paint AC returns.
- Wash sanctuary windows per specifications.

Comparing this to what was achieved by the contractor, the miscellaneous missing items are almost negligible and in no way must detract from the contractor's expertise and reputation. Besides, some of the listed jobs may be extra work not mentioned in the contract, and therefore the contract would be fulfilled.

An update of the ongoing work must regularly be given from the pulpit, written in the bulletin, and/or shown by new photographs posted next to the old ones in the social hall. Restoration Committee members should make themselves available to discuss matters of concern with the parishioners. One must keep in mind that all members volunteer their work, and a certain respect must be shown to their very demanding commitment.

An additional problem always occurs when more money is requested from the church members for extra work. All of a sudden, questions never raised before start to demand an answer:

Why didn't the initial scope of work include this problem?

Was the building engineer or estimator incompetent or just careless?

Why didn't the approved budget cover this expense?

Is the contractor going to take advantage of church generosity and ask for more money for an imaginary task?

Are the committee members going to tolerate such a demand?

If this new problem is real, why not put it out for a new bid?

Will this extra work lead to more "extras"? What are they?

To answer to all these questions is difficult but necessary. Undeniable proof must be provided that the extra work is indeed required. To make an error is only human and, indeed, the estimator may originally have missed the problem. But in most cases, hidden damages are revealed only after taking walls or floors apart. There should not be any argument about this fact, and it is important that a remedy is approved to correct the problem while the work is going on. This is another example of how the contractor's agent/manager intermediates and seals a win-win deal between the church and the workers.

The only negotiation should be over the price. The contractor is already on the job, with scaffoldings in place, workers and tools there, so that contractor is going to take less time and labor to fix the damages. An outside contractor can be asked for an estimate, but the best bet is to let the one already on the job do the work. Most likely the original contractor will ask for less money than anyone else, and the congregation must be made aware of this.

Another problem is the extension of the deadline because of extra work, bad weather, difficulty of the job, or many other solid reasons. While most parishioners understand that unforeseen things may occur, they may resent the idea that Christmas or Easter will find the church still under blue tarps and the altar full of debris. Even more troubling may be that a scheduled wedding cannot be postponed, and the bride is begging that at least the front of the church be ready for a great picture!

As anyone can imagine, to deal with such unforeseen problems requires tact and proper warnings in order to prepare the affected people to accept delays. Once again, good communication between Restoration Committee members and the rest of the people is essential.

The bottom line is: communicate, communicate, communicate! Use the pulpit, church bulletins, local newspapers, church socials, photographs—anything and everything that tells and shows parishioners what is happening and why it needs to happen (see pictures 21 and 22).

Picture 21 (left) and 22. Before and after restoration: the type of photographs to use to keep church members informed.

10

THE POLITICS OF CHANGE

I t seems that everything we do involves politics. If two or more people get together, an opinion arises and politics is in place. A restoration project is no exception. When many people, a wide range of emotions, and a great deal of money are involved, it is inevitable that there are different agendas. Politics can take place inside and outside the church, inside and outside the Restoration Committee.

With regard to the Restoration Committee, all members want to contribute and their noble intentions are obvious. However, some may come with preset ideas about specific issues—not wrong, but different, and with certain quirks. Others may get distracted from the main scope of work and need to be redirected. Some are born leaders, and some are followers. Some are team players, and others are reserved individualists. All act according to their natures.

The leaders are usually knowledgeable, thorough, and well-organized. Because of these good reasons they want to command. The followers are often gentle people who do not want to create any discomfort to the others. Their creativity and professionalism can be superb, yet they would rather give credit to the leader. The team players are the core of any real action, willing to do whatever it takes for the job to be done right. The individualists are originators of many ideas or solutions, and are happy not to be bothered with what others think. So far, these types of members are found in any committee, and their diverse input can be most constructive if properly guided.

The church committee must be aware of some other types of people who can change the course of the restoration.

- ❧ The "careless" member acts too casually, pays little attention to important facts, and proves unrealistic when proposing a budget or a scope of work. He or she will agree with the installation of a one-million-dollar elevator that will travel unnecessarily from the basement to the first floor. But with little knowledge or interest about the real situation, this person will ask for large donations from money-strapped parishioners.

- ❧ Totally opposite is the "cheap" member, who wants the minimum to be done at a minimum expense. This member is always against any spending, and he or she is the most difficult to have a discussion with. To save money is the only concern.

- ❧ Close to this member is the "argumentative" type, for whom everything and everyone is questionable. He or she always second guesses the contractor, who is believed to be overcharging and "trying to take us to the cleaners."

- ❧ The "suspicious" member is the watchdog, eager to report bad news while keeping an eye on everyone, especially on the contractor. He or she is sure there is a "plot" if not against himself or herself, then inside the committee or inside the church.

- ❧ The "overzealous" member is involved with everything, wants to do more than necessary and move things faster. Over-thinking each detail, he or she neglects to look at the big picture and makes everyone nervous. He or she can easily become the "demonstrative" type who takes pleasure in saying "I told you so" when something goes wrong.

❧ The "controlling" member, who may not be the leader, knows everything. He or she may be very knowledgeable but hardly accepts any challenge. This person keeps track of everything, especially money, and is most likely to come to any meeting with his or her own blueprints and list of materials. This is the person who keeps track of the working crew attendance and their job performance, looking for bad workmanship. This is also the one who drives the contractor and the priest/pastor crazy.

❧ The "opportunist" uses his or her role in the committee for personal advantage. While it is not uncommon for committee members to hire the church contractor to work on their personal properties, to ask for "breaks" or "discounts" is not ethical. A gentle reminder during committee meetings should be enough to clarify that kind of situation.

It is generally believed that befriending the contractor means the committee will get more done for the church. In fact, it does the contrary: being overfriendly with contractors can make them believe that they can get away with many wrong things. The best rule is that a contractor is not a friend, but a professional hired to do the job.

Clearly, with all these well-intentioned but different committee members, all kinds of discussions and arguments may occur. Most are constructive, but sometimes the discussions and arguments result in losing track of the original topic or take on other dimensions that result in slowing or even halting the restoration work.

A rule of good politics is that any need to settle internal turmoil among the committee members should be brought in front of the vestry (or whatever the administrative body is called), not to the priest/pastor. In fact, the priest/pastor should never be in a position to take sides or to be involved in contract or money disputes. He or she should stay out of any controversy or dispute.

❀

It is hard to ignore a church restoration, especially in a small town, and for people to talk about it is only natural. However, when people interact with each other, they also interact with the business of the committee and are often suspected of acting in secrecy and serving special interests. To eliminate such gossip, it is important to keep the parishioners and everyone in the general public informed about the progress of the project. Otherwise people will come up with their own version of distorted facts.

One of the common problems the committee is likely to face from "outsiders" is the display of emotional involvement over the reasons for restoration. "The church is forever" seems to be the general thinking and "nothing is wrong with it" seems to be the particular comment. This translates into "no repairs are necessary."

Many people resist changes, particularly when they are about the church. Any upkeeping is almost a sin. "It stayed this way for a hundred years; it can last another hundred years as well!" is the argument. "Air conditioning and a sound system?! No way: this is not a theatre!" is another argument.

When the committee decides to take out certain fixtures like radiators or an outdated lighting system, there is inevitably a group of old-timers who will present the hard-to-defeat plea: "My grandfather did that and it stays that way!" despite its presenting a clear fire code violation or being in danger of collapse. Committee members need to explain to the stubborn "preservationists" that in fact restoration means to preserve the past, while making the church safer and more functional for current use.

Order changes in the middle of the restoration project are probably the most irritating politics of change for most parishioners. Questions like, "Why change the scope of work?" and "Why didn't anyone think about this at the beginning?" have a certain legitimacy. The answer is as follows: "Because restoration is not an exact science, and the work must be adapted to the newly discovered problems." In fact, order changes show that the committee members are observant.

They promptly identified newly arisen situations and dealt with them creatively and wisely for the good of the church.

Another "resistance" church group is usually formed by the new-comers, who basically refuse to donate money because "I just got here. Why should I foot an old bill?" But very rarely do they hang on to that thought, and more likely, the new settlers will want to prove their well wishes with generous offerings.

Nevertheless, there is always a newcomer with new ideas that he or she is determined to defend and implement in the restoration proj-ect. He or she may indeed have good ideas, most likely inspired from the restoration of his or her old church, but no one seems to pay at-tention. The problem seems to be "geopolitical": the person is a new arrival in the parish, while the Restoration Committee is formed of old-timers who have known each other for years. Complaints of the "outsider" will attract partisans who may not like or agree with the committee members, and soon the congregation will face turmoil.

In order to avoid "pro" and "con" groups arising, the Restoration Committee should be very open to suggestions, even perhaps placing a suggestion box to collect ideas and opinions about the project. It is certainly worthwhile to talk to some people who may have something valuable to offer. But there is a certain limit to how open the com-mittee should be to these ideas, which in most cases may be good, but not practical nor financially feasible. Common sense must prevail.

In the end, the team players of the Restoration Committee are the most valuable members who will deal with the politics and prob-lems raised by the long and intricate restoration project. They are the ones who help everyone else focus on what is and is not important, what the priorities are, and the proper order of the jobs. Some of them must inspect the job site, some may re-inspect it, and all find-ings must be carefully analyzed and discussed with the contractor in a professional manner.

Outside the Restoration Committee there can be forces that greatly influence its activity. Some priests/pastors become the CEO of their churches and decide to run them as corporations. In no time, especially newly installed priests/pastors begin to create grounds for a corporate structure. The church secretary may now have his or her own secretaries, and the space might be divided by new offices with names and titles on the doors. Part-timers are hired to do what volunteers used to do. A select group of advisors meet in private with the eager priest/pastor, and soon bills start to pour into the church mail box. Architects, interior decorators, financial advisors and many others who began to do consulting work for the church become regular employees.

Very often a church member who is an investor offers to put the endowment money in the stock market. Although in good times the investment return may be great, in bad times the money needed for restoration or other improvements can be gone. To compensate for that loss, the priest/pastor sends fund-raisers to call or to knock on the doors of the parishioners, who may already be swimming in debt.

We do live in fast-changing times when everything we need is within the touch of a button, but the old-fashioned way of worshipping and conducting business within the church is still a good policy. In fact, why change something that worked for hundreds of years? Restoring the church is one piece of church business that should not be too different in procedure from what our grandparents used to do —except using new construction tools.

Politics has always been around and will continue to be, for good reasons. One solution is to put together a group of people who love to help the church and want to leave a good deed behind them. The prayers of future generations will unknowingly include them as well.

11

CELEBRATION

The completion of a major church restoration is an event that happens once or twice in a century. The majestic white steeple or the glowing golden dome, the newly refinished large entrance doors, the immaculate siding, and the sparkling windows ask for acknowledgment. Parishioners, who have stood outside while the church was closed, encircled with scaffoldings, and surrounded by debris, are anxious to inspect their refurbished house of worship. And the community at large has been driving by the church and has watched it emerge—like a butterfly from its cocoon.

A celebration is called for!

The celebration begins with the first church service when the church is re-opened.

If weather permits, many times the celebration immediately precedes the service. In front of the church, the priest/pastor delivers a short speech of thanks and a prayer to the parishioners who are waiting to enter the church and are lined up in processional formation. The church bell begins to toll. It is an emotional moment, with the church flags waving high, the robed choir singing with voices that reach heaven, and happy parishioners with their friends, ceremoniously entering the glistening sanctuary (see picture 23).

Everything looks new, yet everything is in the same place —but now repaired, looking better, and carefully refurbished. The floors no longer squeak, and the aisle carpet is just the

Picture 23. A church celebrates its restoration.

right color and softness. Everyone sits on shiny pews that have new velvety, comfortable cushions. The hymnal books may be new or rebound. The chandeliers add light from the sparkling clean windows, and that light reflects in the restored walls, ceiling, and floral moldings, all with a beauty that had been hidden beneath grime and age-damage. The altar rose window looks glorious with colorful details once again alive and meaningful. People continuously look around with wonder and joy, while the organist and the choir finish their introductory hymn.

Everything and everybody looks better than before. It is solemnity at its best.

The service flows as usual, but with a difference in ambience. The sermon may deal with resurrection and giving, balancing scripture with the "resurrection" of the church structure and the giving of those who made it possible. The minister, another clergy person, or a designated guest (possibly the leader of the Restoration Committee) may point to different areas or objects that offered a challenge during the restoration and briefly explain how the problem was solved. Some unexpected problems may be recalled in a humorous way, noting God's help in resolving the issues. Restoration Committee members or other key people involved in the restoration may be invited to stand up and be acknowledged for their unpaid but rewarding efforts. Sometimes a tour of the restoration is offered, with mention of where to meet and who will lead the tour.

Following the service, one or two Restoration Committee members might stand with the priest/pastor at the doorway to shake hands with the people leaving the sanctuary. This gives the parishioners an opportunity to say thank you to representatives of those who have worked so diligently to complete a difficult and complicated project.

Everyone may be invited to the fellowship or social hall after the service for coffee and donuts, where there is usually a display of photographs showing the process of the restoration. Many times a real feast with an appetizing spread of dishes is planned.

The celebration party requires advance planning by the Restoration Committee, beginning several months prior to the anticipated completion of the restoration work. Two groups need to be informed about the party: the parishioners and the general community. The factors that need to be considered by the Restoration Committee are:

- The date
- The exact nature of the festivities
- People to be specially acknowledged during the celebration
- The precise locale of the festivities
- Media participation

EXPECTED COMPLETION DATE

Timing is crucial. Be certain the restoration is complete before you announce a celebration function. The Restoration Committee will have a projected completion date from the contractor. Have a tentative date for the celebration so the committee can start planning, but wait to announce the actual date until the scaffolding has been taken away and all the last-minute fine-tuning is finished.

EXACT NATURE OF THE FESTIVITIES

The celebration is usually a party or a series of parties. There may be a breakfast, luncheon, or dinner for the Restoration Committee, hosted by the priest/pastor. Often there is a function following the first Sunday church services. Sometimes there is a party arranged for an evening. Food and beverages are usually provided by church members. These may be coffee, tea, donuts, muffins, and coffee cake; sandwiches and soft drinks; a catered dinner party or buffet.

PEOPLE TO BE ACKNOWLEDGED

This is the time for the priest/pastor to thank the hard-working Restoration Committee! It is also the time to herald the donors who made the restoration possible, from the dollar contributors to the benefactors who gave thousands of dollars and those who supplied goods and materials. All of these people should be acknowledged and thanked from the pulpit and in the church bulletins.

The Restoration Committee needs to determine how exactly it wants to make its thanks to major benefactors. Perhaps a donor is responsible for something specific—the stained glass window or the rebound hymnals. Perhaps the donor has contributed a large sum of money. Sometimes special plaques are made and placed in the parish house or in a section of the sanctuary. Sometimes a gift is presented to the donor—a beautifully framed photograph of the restored church, with an embossed thank-you plaque. There are many options from simple to elaborate. What is important is recognition and appreciation.

LOCALE OF THE FESTIVITIES

The Restoration Committee decides the locale that is best suited for festivities for their parishioners and community. Weather and time of year need to be considered. A party may be held in the parish house if there is sufficient room; it may spill from the parish parlor to other adjacent rooms; it may be both in the parish parlor and under a tarp or tent outside, or on the church green or the green across the street (with back-up plans for inclement weather). It is not uncommon to have the restoration celebration party set up in the middle of a church fair with rented equipment to entertain the children; a big band playing "oldies" to entertain the adults; games; and lots and lots of food, sometimes including barbecue or a pig roast.

MEDIA PARTICIPATION

With regard to announcing the restoration and the open celebration party through the press, a public relations executive makes these suggestions:

Two weeks before the party date:

- E-mail or hand-deliver the press release to the local newspaper(s).

- Include a cover note describing the photographs that can be provided.

- Follow up with a phone call the next day and discuss with the newspaper reporter which photographs may be desired and in what form (print or digital).

- Be sure to invite the reporter to the celebration.

- Let the reporter know of any "important" people coming to the celebration party so the newspaper can consider sending a photographer as well. A photo in the newspaper of the pastor, the Restoration Committee, and major contributors is a good thing!

The potential number of people attending and the ebb and flow of the guests need to be taken into account. It is also important to set a "start" and "end" time so that people can plan their own and their children's schedules. And, if the event is outside, be sure to say the festivities are taking place "rain or shine" or give a rain date.

Usually there is no RSVP for church celebrations, as everyone is invited and it is hoped that many will attend! The Restoration Committee has to do its best to estimate the number of people for the food and beverage planners.

Some committees have a small, more formal dinner for the committee itself and major donors. This is usually in addition to the large, all-invited celebration party.

The general public and parishioners are also informed about the party through the media, which should also cover the restoration itself. These two events can be combined for the local newspapers.

Typically, at least a month prior to the anticipated completion of the restoration, the church public relations person or a designated member of the Restoration Committee begins preparing an announcement for the local newspaper (see sidebar on writing a press release). Plan to ask a reporter from each local newspaper to write a story about how the restoration took place, illustrating the story with photographs, and inviting everyone in the community to attend a celebration. Count on the local politicians and their handshakes.

How to write a press release:

The press release is a news announcement, so the most important news must be presented first. In the case of a church restoration, that means the first paragraph says there will be a celebration, the date, time, place (with address), and the news that the celebration is open to the public.

The second paragraph gives a brief history of the church—how old it is, if and when there was an earlier restoration, what was needed in this restoration, who did the restoration, how it was paid for (naming major contributors unless they want to remain anonymous), how long it took, and any other "interesting" news.

The third paragraph heralds the sparkling changes—any new additions (lighting, air conditioning, new or refurbished pews).

The fourth paragraph returns to the celebration, providing more details about the event itself—if there will be escorted tours of the church, an invitation to view "a history of the restoration panel" on display in the parish house, the refreshments that will be served and who is providing them, and so on.

The release should be no longer than one and one-half typed pages. There should be several photographs—print and digital, if possible—of the restoration in progress, as well as a couple of close-ups of special restoration projects (for example, the steeple or dome, the new front doors), as well as a photograph of the full front view of the church.

Consider as you are planning:

- Options for bad weather
- Food and beverages, preparation, delivery, table setup, tablecloths, utensils, caterers/equipment suppliers
- Entertainment: music, activities for children
- Childcare center
- Location to position a mural showing progression of restoration
- Location to post "Special Thanks" poster or mural, with names and/or photos of donors
- Parking
- Access for infirm or disabled persons
- Possible need for a microphone and/or audiovisual (AV) equipment (there may be video of the restoration that can be shown during the party)
- Electrical and other special equipment needs
- Closets/coat racks
- Name tags
- Formal words by the priest/pastor (microphone) or informal mingling
- A commemorative give-away card showing the church when first built (and year) and the restored church (and year restoration was completed)

Remember, any type of festivity is a celebration as it marks the completion of the restoration project. A party may be large or small, attended by dozens or hundreds. Whatever it is, it honors something that is not likely to happen again in the lifetime of anyone who attends. The celebration party is ephemeral, a moment in time—but a moment of joy. What is lasting is the legacy of hard-working, dedicated people who did their jobs, served their faith, and honored their church by re-creating a solidly constructed place of worship. They helped the church building resurrect through restoration!

A f t e r w o r d

There is always a mystical beauty and a respectful feeling that an old church imposes on us, just like a military uniform that is never out of fashion and never loses its importance. The old churches instantly recall the glory of a bygone era we call the "good old days," and people fiercely defend this connection with the past. Indeed, the postcard picture of a church building endures in communities throughout the entire world.

Yet a church is more than a picturesque building: it is a timeless functional temple that connects millennia and generations. It provides people the sanctity of baptism, communion, and marriage. If offers a place to educate children and to meditate. It is, finally, the last stop for many before their eternal departure. Whatever its style and design, a church always looks special. Even between skyscrapers, a church building stands tall and grand, however elaborate or simple its actual structure. Its presence can induce an instant change of attitude from passersby: from bitterness to happiness, from despair to optimism. For many, a visit to a church means communication with the Ultimate Authority who provides hope and peace of mind. Anyone working in church restoration must keep these things in focus and conduct work that respects and preserves the mythical aura that is intrinsic to the church.

Churches are probably the most untouched link with the American prerevolutionary past, still standing proud to engage people's imagination of a bygone era. Their stunning architecture has lasted as a testimony of care and pride, for it commands an instant respect for the hard work and deep faith of the American pioneers and forebears. An old church provides a unique feeling of spirituality and induces reflection about a simpler world that produced with primitive tools such great landmarks on a virgin land.

It is a blessing that so many churches were already built. With today's costly labor and materials, lack of old-fashioned craftsmen, and endless state and town building codes, building a new church seems almost an impossibility.

To make sure these architectural monuments will last in perpetuity for generations to cherish and enjoy, their restoration is a civic and moral duty. My hope is that this book provides Restoration Committees with basic and practical advice and ideas for working with restorers to do the right job.

For inquiries, please feel free to write to me at Ion Grumeza, c/o The Pilgrim Press, 700 Prospect Avenue, Cleveland, Ohio 44115, or to e-mail me (churchrestorer@aol.com).

Bibliography

Haerer, Alfred. *Building Construction Fundamentals*. Cincinnati: The National Underwriter Company, 1970.

Lawrence, Mike, and Derek Bradford, eds. *The Complete Home Renovation Manual*. New York: Smithmark Publishers, 1993.

The Old House Journal —1990s.

Poore, Patricia, ed. *The Old-House Journal Guide to Restoration*. New York: Dutton Books, 1992.

State Building Code, 1999 Connecticut Supplement.

Toy, Sidney. *Castles: Their Construction and History*. New York: Dover Publications, 1985.

U.S. Department of Labor, Occupational Safety and Health Administration, Construction Industry Duges, 1998.

White, Anthony, and Bruce Robertson. *Architecture & Ornament*. New York: Design Press, 1990.